HAUNTED
BATON ROUGE

HAUNTED BATON ROUGE

BUD STEED

PHOTOGRAPHY BY HOPE STEED KENNEDY

HAUNTED America

Published by Haunted America
A Division of The History Press
Charleston, SC 29403
www.historypress.net

Copyright © 2013 by Bud Steed
All rights reserved

First published 2013

Manufactured in the United States

ISBN 978.1.60949.862.7

Library of Congress CIP data applied for.

CONTENTS

Contents

ACKNOWLEDGEMENTS

This book is dedicated to my wife, Jennifer Lynn Steed. Over the years that we have spent together, she has never lost faith in me—even when I have lost faith in myself. She has always been my constant cheerleader, offering words of encouragement and a hug and a kiss in those moments when I doubted myself and my abilities. She is my rock, and I love her for it. To my kids—David, Sean, Ciara Jo and Kerra Lynn—I thank you for your understanding and patience when I was too busy writing and researching to throw the baseball or football with you or to simply hang out and watch *Tinker Bell and the Great Fairy Rescue* with you (after about the fortieth time, I can effectively quote most of the parts by heart). Watching you guys grow and become the fine young men and ladies that you are is truly gratifying and a testament to your mother's hard work. It's not easy being my kids, but you manage it well, and I love you all more than life itself.

To my eldest daughter, Bobbi Jo, I miss you constantly, and not a day passes that I don't think of you or wonder what your life would have been like. Rest in peace, sweetie. We all love and miss you.

To my good friend David E. Harkins, the founder and director of our paranormal investigation team, the Ozarks Paranormal Society, and an accomplished writer in his own right (author of *Haunted Graveyards of the Ozarks*), thanks for always having my back and for always being ready to help, even on short notice.

To my parents, Merlin Sr. and Rose Steed, I thank you for never giving up on me even though I gave you ample reasons to do so. Your encouragement, love and forgiveness over the years has been much appreciated, and I can only hope that I end up being half the parent to my children that each of you were to me. I love you guys.

And lastly, to my friend and physician, Dr. Gabrielle Curtis, I thank you for your excellent care and for managing to keep me alive in spite of myself and my poor adherence to your prescribed medical recommendations. I would certainly hate to have me for a patient.

I would also like to acknowledge those who have offered help during the researching and writing of this book. Thanks to my niece Hope Steed Kennedy for taking the time out of her busy schedule to take some of the photos I needed for this book. Her knowledge of the Baton Rouge area was extremely valuable in getting just the right photos in the shortest amount of time possible. A multi-talented young lady, she will go far in this world if she continues to chase after her passions. Also, thanks to my wife, Jennifer, for helping proofread the rough draft of this book, for keeping me on task and on schedule with words of encouragement and the occasional "Aren't you supposed to be writing?" and, most importantly, for keeping the kids quiet and occupied so that I could write. Thanks to Becky LeJeune at The History Press for all of your concern and understanding regarding some medical issues that slowed up the delivery of this manuscript. I also appreciate everyone else at The History Press for all of the hard work in bringing this book and my previous ones to life.

Introduction

Is Baton Rouge Haunted?

Baton Rouge is an eclectic mixture of both modern and historic perched alongside the Mississippi River about eighty miles north of New Orleans. While much has been written about the paranormal aspects of New Orleans, I found it strange that Baton Rouge has very little in writing about ghosts and hauntings, especially given the age of the city and its history. My younger brother, Walt Steed, a twenty-plus-year resident of the Baton Rouge area, first brought it to my attention when I was discussing upcoming book projects with him one night. "You should write a book about Baton Rouge," he said. "There are a lot of haunted places here, but no one writes about them." A little bit of research revealed that stories were plentiful, although they were told mainly by word of mouth, passed down through families and friends. That revealed to me that while there might be a shortage of ghostly accounts in writing, there certainly is no shortage of them being told among the residents of the city. Wherever I went while researching this book, I was met with dozens and dozens of friendly people who were quite eager to share their stories of ghosts and hauntings, willingly answering my inquiries with enthusiasm and pride in their city and heritage. It's no secret to the people of the Baton Rouge area that they live in a truly haunted place, and they are no different than their counterparts all across the country—they all love to tell and listen to a good ghost story about their hometown.

Armed with that knowledge, I set out to research and document some of the stories that were told to me, looking, as usual, for the historical connection. (Anyone who has read my previous books, *Haunted Natchez Trace* and *Haunted Mississippi Gulf Coast*, knows how much emphasis I place on the history surrounding the hauntings.) To my way of thinking, each ghost story and legend had its start somewhere, usually in a factual occurrence that either grew with each telling or from which the actual ghost story stemmed. Some of the stories I discovered were nothing more than urban legends and could not be confirmed as stemming from an actual event. Others, however, were easily matched to actual happenings, and while in some cases nothing more than the event itself could be verified, in others, names and dates were easy to match to the story. Those are the ones that quickly catch my attention, both as a paranormal investigator/researcher and as a writer, as those are the stories from which you naturally gravitate from writer to investigator, delving into the story armed with the names and facts to try and document some hard evidence to substantiate the story. I wasn't able to investigate each place or story, as neither family obligations nor finances would allow that much time away from home, but I was able to look into a few that I found to be fascinating in both a historical and a paranormal aspect.

I also decided to cast a wide loop, so to speak, around the Baton Rouge area and look into stories and places out to a distance of fifteen miles from the Baton Rouge city limits. Since the metropolitan area covers such a wide amount of space, I thought that it would be beneficial to include some of the stories from the outlying areas. Even though these towns have names and identities of their own, they are still referenced by many as simply being a part of "BR" or "the Rouge."

So is Baton Rouge a haunted city? Do ghosts and specters walk the streets and the hallways of its buildings? In my opinion, the answer to those questions is most definitely yes! My answer is based both on the amount of stories there are as well as the history of the area.

A Brief History of the "Red Stick"

Baton Rouge, which literally means "Red Stick," was reportedly given its name by Pierre Le Moyne, the Sieur d'Iberville. Le Moyne, who was instrumental in establishing colonies for the French all along the Gulf Coast area, was exploring the Mississippi River when he came across a reddish

A cannon monument overlooking the river. *Photo by Hope Steed Kennedy.*

cypress pole upon which hung the carcasses of bloody animals and fish. This pole marked the boundary between the Houma tribe and the Bayou Goula tribe and was actually situated on Istrouma Bluff, the first bluff that one would come to going upriver that was high enough to ensure that the marker wouldn't be washed away by flooding.

It is now thought from the excavation of mounds left by the indigenous peoples and from further research of surrounding areas that the land that now comprises Baton Rouge has been inhabited since nearly 8000 BCE. The three remaining mounds within the city are believed to have been built by more advanced peoples around 5000–3500 BCE, and while not believed to have been used as burial mounds, many researchers believe that they were used for religious and social purposes. That means that the area around Baton Rouge has been lived on for at least ten thousand years or so. But the real documented history from which a lot of the ghost stories and legends stem from began around 1719 with the establishment of a fort at the location. Baton Rouge would grow quickly to become one of the more prominent French settlements in the area.

In 1755, in what would become known as the Great Expulsion, British soldiers deported around eleven thousand French Acadians from Acadia, which is now Nova Scotia, sending them back to France, where many were later relocated to La Louisiane. A good number would settle in the area near Baton Rouge, an area that would come to be known as Acadiana. The people eventually became known as Cajuns. By maintaining their diverse culture of food, music and devotion to the Catholic religion, they have evolved into their own subculture and have been instrumental in making the area famous.

The Treaty of Paris, signed on February 10, 1763, saw all of the French holdings in America pass into British hands. The settlement slowly developed as a town under the British due to its significance as the southwestern-most outpost of the British Americas. Unfortunately for Britain, its control of the area was to be short-lived. When the American Revolution broke out, Baton Rouge stayed loyal to the crown, but in 1778, France declared war on Britain, as did Spain in 1779. That same year, the Spanish governor of New Orleans, Don Bernardo de Galvez, led a force of around 1,400 troops and a few rebellious British subjects and captured the newly constructed Fort New Richmond in the Battle of Baton Rouge after just three hours of artillery shelling. This had the distinction of being the only Revolutionary War battle to be fought outside the boundaries of the original thirteen colonies. Galvez would later capture both Mobile and Pensacola, ending the British presence along the gulf. In 1810, the land would pass on to American hands after rebels overcame the Spanish garrison at Baton Rouge, establishing the Republic of West Florida, which existed for a mere ninety days before being annexed into the United States. On April 30, 1812, Louisiana was admitted to the Union as the eighteenth state.

Because of Baton Rouge's strategic location along the Mississippi River, the U.S. Army built a series of buildings between 1819 and 1822 that, due to their pentagonal layout, became known as the Pentagon Barracks. The barracks were large enough to house approximately one thousand troops, and with the building of the Baton Rouge Arsenal and Ordnance Depot, Baton Rouge became a major outpost on the Mississippi River. It was so important, in fact, that when the Civil War broke out, the state of Louisiana, after secession from the union, seized the barracks and arsenal and turned them over to the Confederacy. The Confederates would evacuate Baton Rouge in April 1862 after the Battle of New Orleans, and Union troops would move in and occupy the city in May 1862, holding onto it throughout the war, even through one attempt by the Confederates, the Battle of Baton Rouge (August 1862), to retake it. The town was severely damaged during the battle, although not to the extent of other cities that were major conflict areas during the war. Baton Rouge did supply nearly one third of its male

Aerial view of the Pentagon Barracks. *Courtesy Library of Congress, Prints and Photographs Division, HABS LA, 17-BATRO, 8-1.*

THE BATTLE OF BATON ROUGE, L$^\text{A}$ AUG. 4$^\text{TH}$ 1862.

Battle of Baton Rouge, August 4, 1862, from a Currier and Ives print. *Courtesy Library of Congress, Prints and Photographs Division, LC-USZ62-60328.*

population to the Southern cause with the formation of several volunteer companies such as the Pelican Rifles, the Creole Guards, the Baton Rouge Fencibles and the Delta Rifles.

After the war, the period of Reconstruction brought many changes to the city, which saw many freedmen moving from the rural areas all over the South to the cities as they sought to escape white control and find better jobs and educational opportunities. By 1880, the population of the city was 60 percent black, and it would take until 1920 before the white population would exceed even 50 percent. The city would grow despite racial segregation and Jim Crow laws, which bred conflict and racial hatred among those in both races. And in the early part of the twentieth century, new business and development, along with the arrival of the Louisville, New Orleans and Texas Railway, saw much new opportunity for the city. With the railroad and its strategic location along the river, the city became a large industrialized area. Standard Oil began building processing facilities, with many other petroleum and chemical companies following suit. Safety standards weren't always the highest back then, and many deaths occurred during the early years in both the plants and the refineries. Stories are still told about some of the unfortunate souls who go to work at the plants each day, many years after they met their untimely demise on the job.

Baton Rouge weathered the Great Depression with a large public works project. The building of the new Louisiana State Capitol building was directed by Governor Huey P. Long in 1932 and was considered to be a symbol of modernization and growth. Also built around the same time were the Louisiana Institute for the Blind and the School for the Deaf and Dumb, both providing much-needed services for the state and seen as signs of the city's progressiveness.

During World War II, the city thrived, with the military demanding increased production of petroleum and chemicals to be used in the war effort. This increased production would continue after the war and contributed to the steady growth of the city, helping to firmly establish it as an economic center on the Mississippi River.

In the early 1950s, the Civil Rights Movement hit Baton Rouge when black citizens of the city organized an eight-day boycott of the municipal bus system. Volunteers provided free rides, organized through churches, which effectively hit the bus system where it hurt—in their coffers. Nearly 80 percent of the bus riders were black, so the municipal bus system suffered a significant loss of income during the boycott. As a result, the Baton Rouge City Council was forced to revisit its ordinance that called for segregated seating on the buses. By 1960, student sit-ins hit the city when seven Southern University students were arrested for staging a sit-in at a Kress lunch counter. The next day saw another sit-in that resulted in the arrests of nine more Southern University students, and this led to a march by more than three thousand students on the state capitol to protest segregation and to call for the release of the arrested students. More sit-ins and protests followed, culminating in a protest of more than one thousand students at the state capitol on December 15, 1961. Police attacked the students with tear gas and dogs, arresting fifty of them. Thousands rallied in support of the arrested students at the Southern University campus, leading SU officials to close the campus early for the holidays to avoid any further protests. The end of segregation and the enforcement of civil rights did not come easy to Baton Rouge. Hatred based on the color of a person's skin was ingrained in the social order, but as with most things in life, eventually the good will prevail. Old attitudes replaced with more progressive ones, and today people of all racial and ethnic backgrounds call the city home.

A boom in the petrochemical industries in the 1970s caused more growth and expansion in the city, giving way to suburban sprawl as more people and businesses moved to the outskirts of the metropolitan area. Continued building booms, new technology businesses and improvements geared to the quality of life of the residents have seen Baton Rouge take its place at the forefront as one of the fastest growing metropolitan areas in the state.

The history, architecture and diverse cultures that make up this city have contributed to the formation of the city motto: "Authentic Louisiana at Every Turn." It is a motto that sums up the vibe of the city quite well.

The Ghosts and Hauntings of Baton Rouge

Now that you are acquainted with a little history of the city, let's delve into the hauntings and ghost stories associated with the area. I have listed these accountings of the paranormal in the order in which I personally found them to be most interesting without trying to group them by location within the city. You might not agree with me on the interest level of each story, but please indulge me a bit and I assure you that you won't be disappointed in the end result.

I think I should also add that these are simply ghost stories and legends that have been told and retold over the years, and regardless of how much documented history might be included with each story, without investigating each occurrence individually to try and obtain documented proof that the story is true, partially true or just an urban legend, they should be taken with a "grain of salt." Should any novice investigators decide after reading these stories to go out and investigate their validity, please be sure and follow these simple rules:

1) Always obtain permission first and never ever trespass.
2) Take plenty of backup batteries.
3) "If you carry it in, you carry it out." (In other words, never leave trash behind.)
4) For safety's sake, never investigate alone. Always make sure another person who you are *not* investigating with knows where you are going to be and establish a check-in time with them.
5) Never destroy, vandalize or remove anything from the investigation site that does not belong to you. When you are investigating, you are representing not only yourselves but the rest of us in this field as well.
6) Above all else, have fun!

CHAPTER 1

THE GHOSTS OF THE PENTAGON BARRACKS

The Baton Rouge Barracks, nicknamed the "Pentagon Barracks" due to the layout of the buildings, were built over a period of about six years, from 1819 to 1825. James Gadsden, a captain in the U.S. Army, designed the two-story brick buildings and oversaw their construction. The buildings were laid out forming four sides of a regular pentagon, with an additional building housing a commissary and warehouse making up the fifth side. The commissary building was torn down not long after its construction due to an oversight in construction that rendered it unstable and unusable; however, the name Pentagon Barracks would live on.

In January 1861, the State of Louisiana seized the barracks and the adjoining arsenal from the Union troops who occupied it in a bloodless attack and turned over the operation of the complex to the Confederate States of America. Confederate troops were housed at the barracks until they evacuated Baton Rouge in April 1862 during the Battle of New Orleans. By May of that year, the barracks and all of Baton Rouge were in the hands of the Union army. The Confederates staged an attempt to regain the city in August. About six thousand Confederate troops attacked just north of the city and were defeated by about eighteen thousand firmly entrenched Union soldiers. The town was damaged badly, and several civilians, as well as numerous soldiers from both sides, including Union general Thomas Williams, were killed during the attack. The Union army would rename the facility Fort Williams in General Williams's honor. By 1884, the barracks were no longer in use by the

Southwest façade of the North Building of the Pentagon Barracks. *Courtesy Library of Congress, Prints and Photographs Division, HABS LA, 17-BATRO, 8-14.*

army. After a resolution passed by the General Assembly of Louisiana, the property and buildings were allocated to Louisiana State University. The school would gain full possession of the property around 1886, and it would remain there until moving to its new campus in 1926. For the most part, the barracks would fluctuate between usage and abandonment up until 1976, when the property was transferred back to the State of Louisiana and then placed on the National Register of Historic Places. Work would begin on the buildings shortly after that, and today they house the Pentagon Barracks Museum, the lieutenant governor's offices and private apartments for the use of state legislators when they are in the city. Lots of stories have circulated about the barracks over the years, and several legislators have moved out of the apartments due to strange occurrences, preferring to obtain their own quarters rather than stay at the converted barracks.

Archway at the Northeast Building of the Pentagon Barracks. *Courtesy Library of Congress, Prints and Photographs Division, HAB LA, 17-BATRO, 8-12.*

SADIE'S GHOST

After the Civil War, the facility and grounds would continue to house American troops and, by all accounts, was the site of the rape and murder of a young black woman referenced only as Sadie. Said to have taken place around 1868, the perpetrator was unfortunately never caught. As the story goes, a group of soldiers was returning from the city after enjoying an evening pass when they happened to hear the bloodcurdling screams of a woman coming from the woods near the barracks. After investigating, they discovered the body of a young black woman, her clothing torn and partially removed, who had been stabbed several times in a rather brutal fashion. The stab wounds were to her lower stomach and genitalia, and her throat had been savagely slashed. Boot prints and one brass button were reportedly found near her body, the button being firmly grasped in her hand as if she had ripped it from her attacker's shirt in the final struggle for her life. The button was recognized as coming from a military uniform, and the barracks were searched in hopes that by finding it, they would find the killer. But the uniform was never found; it was most likely disposed of by the murderer as he fled the scene. The case was closed due to a lack of leads, although I would suspect that given the era in which it happened and the fact that the victim was a young black woman, not much effort was expended to find the killer.

Apparently, the young murder victim, Sadie, wasn't satisfied with the results of the case, because for several years afterward, stories were circulated about a young black girl who could be seen walking the grounds of the barracks, clutching her stomach. Thinking that someone was in distress, a trooper or two would go to investigate only to see the woman fade from sight. One particular incident that was rumored to have taken place was her appearance to the commander of the troops stationed at the barracks. While lying in bed one night, he was awakened by someone standing at the foot of his bed. Thinking an orderly had entered the room due to some difficulty that required his attention, he sat up and asked what was wrong. Getting no reply, he asked several more times, still getting no reply. Aggravated at what he thought was an insubordinate soldier, he got up and struck a match to light the lamp next to his bed. It was in the light of the match that he realized that it wasn't a soldier at all but rather a young black girl. Confused, he finished lighting the lamp and then directed his full attention to the woman. That is when he saw that she was drenched in blood from the waist down, her eyes staring vacantly at him. The legend holds that he rushed to her side, thinking she had been injured and wandered in seeking help, while shouting for his orderly to come help. As he reached her side, she slowly began to fade from sight and took on an almost luminous cast. As both he and the freshly arrived orderly watched in horror, she turned and walked through the wall, disappearing from sight. Both men are reported to have rushed outside, but no trace of the woman could be found. When the men returned to the commander's quarters, no trace of blood could be found on the floors, walls or bedding. This happened for several nights in a row (causing the officer great mental stress, I'm sure), and on the last night she appeared, he had his orderly firmly set in the corner of the room keeping watch. When she appeared, the officer summoned the courage to ask her what she wanted and why she was tormenting him so, to which she uttered just one word: "Help." Perhaps Sadie thought that a direct plea to the officer in charge might get her the justice she never got, bringing peace to her soul. Either way, she never appeared again to the officer, although for many years, she was seen walking the grounds of the barracks clutching her midsection as if in distress.

THE SHADOW MAN

When the state took over the barracks and started renovating the property, stories were told of things happening at the buildings that, while not too terribly spooky, were nonetheless quite strange to the workers. There were stories of disappearing tools that would suddenly reappear out of thin air; boards that were nailed firmly in place unexplainably falling, the nails still driven through them; and lunches that would disappear only to be found outside, the contents of the lunch boxes and bags thrown about the area. More than one worker saw what was described as "shooting balls of light" darting about the rooms during the renovation. But one story stands out above the rest in relation to the apartments where the state legislators live while in the capital: the story of the Shadow Man.

I was first told this story over twenty years ago while in Baton Rouge visiting my brother. While waiting for him to finish up at work, I struck up a conversation with an older gentleman who was waiting to pick up his son from work. He was an extremely nice guy who loved to talk, and he told me that he had previously worked as a maintenance man at the state capitol grounds for a number of years before retiring. We both shared a love of history, and I was interested in his perspective of the Civil War period since he was black and his family had lived there for several generations. The conversation moved to the history of the Pentagon Barracks, and he shared a lot of information with me about the facility that he had learned while working there, most specifically that the place was haunted and quite spooky, especially at night. Although he confessed straight off that he believed in ghosts and didn't want anything to do with them, the things he encountered at the complex didn't really terrify him to the point that he was afraid to work in any of the buildings—with the exception of the Shadow Man at the apartments. He said that the shadowy figure was very menacing and that his one encounter with him was what made him decide to quit the maintenance job and seek early retirement.

He told me that he had been getting one of the apartments ready for an incoming legislator, just making sure that everything was freshly painted and that any items on the work order were completed. Working late so that he could get everything finished that day, he noticed that it was starting to get dark outside, so he turned on the lights in the room where he was working and continued on with what he was doing. He said he kept catching something moving in the shadows of the adjoining room out of the corner of his eye. Thinking that a co-worker had entered the apartment, he called out to them. Getting no reply, he stopped what he was doing and went into the next room, turning on the lights as he entered. No sooner had he turned on the lights than all the light bulbs in the room surged brightly and then immediately burned out. Thinking it was a power surge, he flipped the light switch back off and made a mental note to change the light bulbs before he left that evening. As he turned to leave, he saw what appeared to be the figure of a man dart along the wall, keeping to the shadows. Knowing that no one was there, as he had an unobstructed view of the entire room in the moments before the lights burned out, he thought that his eyes were playing tricks on him. After all, it had been a long, busy day and he was pretty tired, so he shrugged it off and returned to what he was doing.

He finished painting the trim around the doorway, cleaned up the paintbrushes and moved to the next item on the list: repairing the plumbing under the bathroom sink. He lay down on the floor and moved into the cabinet a ways so that he could better access the water lines and was working on removing the leaking line from the sink when he noticed that it was getting darker inside the small bathroom. About that time, he said it felt like something heavy was suddenly sitting on his chest and that he couldn't move. As he started to kick his legs about in a panic while trying to get out from under the sink, something latched onto his lower leg and dragged him from under the cabinet. That is when he first laid eyes on the Shadow Man. Standing over him was a black mass in the shape of a man's body but without any visible features; no eyes, no mouth—just a solid outline of a large man standing over him. He said he was instantly petrified with fear as it was nothing that he had ever seen before and the vibe it was giving off was one of extreme malice. The thing stepped over him, bent down and grabbed him by the collar of his shirt and dragged him out of the bathroom, down the hallway and into the main room, where the survival instinct of "fight or flight" kicked in and he started to struggle to get free and to get on his feet. He swiveled around and kicked out with his legs only to see, to his horror, his legs pass right through the legs of the shadowy figure, leaving a "trail of black smoke that sucked back into place as soon as my legs finished passing through it."

Finding his voice, he started shouting for it to let him go, creating "quite a ruckus," as he put it. His shouts and screams attracted the attention of another worker who was working in the building. As the man rushed into the room, thinking that his friend had been injured, he drew up sharply at the sight of the Shadow Man gripping the collar of his co-worker, his eyes wide with disbelief. About that time, the Shadow Man uttered an angry hiss, at which point he physically slung the man by the collar across the room at the co-worker and then turned and darted into the next room, back into the shadows. Regaining his feet, the man looked at his co-worker, at which point both men broke out into a dead run, not stopping until they were completely free of the building.

A second-floor porch at the Pentagon Barracks. *Courtesy Library of Congress, Prints and Photographs Division, HABS LA ,17-BATRO, 8-9.*

That neither of the men went back to the building that night is a given. They instead waited until the next morning to reenter the apartment by the light of day, and even then it was only to quickly finish the water line while the other stood guard. They then gathered up their tools, my acquaintance retiring from his job shortly thereafter. He told me that that was the most terrified he had ever been in his life and that he was sure that if his co-worker hadn't rushed in when he did, he wouldn't be alive today to tell me the story. That the Shadow Man was bent on causing him harm was plain to the man, and he even admitted to not being able to sleep well at night, as he was constantly waking and searching the shadows of his bedroom for the Shadow Man. Several other people have reported seeing a shadow figure in and around the apartments, but to my knowledge, no one has have ever had an encounter like that related to me by the gentleman I visited with that day. What it was he couldn't venture to say, only that it was powerful and very menacing. I asked him if he had ever thought about going back there some night and seeing if it was still there, to which he gave me an incredulous look and stated quite emphatically, "Not ever in this lifetime. My momma didn't raise no fool."

CHAPTER 2
THE OLD ARSENAL MUSEUM

Located on the grounds of the state capitol, the Old Arsenal Powder Magazine is one of the surviving structures of Louisiana's largest military complex. Left neglected for years, the structure has been restored and turned into a museum depicting the history of the arsenal.

Arsenals were located all over the United States in the nineteenth century, stretching from border to border. And much like the current military bases we have today, arsenals of that time housed troops, supplies, large amounts of powder and ammunition and everything necessary to operate a military post.

The Baton Rouge arsenal contained a large ordnance warehouse in its early years, but in about 1838, the powder magazine was constructed to provide a safer storage facility for thousands of pounds of gunpowder. Constructed of thick brick walls, the interior contained vaults that held the powder. The magazine was surrounded by a high, thick brick wall that helped provide additional safety for the surrounding area and buildings in the event of a mishap. The arsenal was placed in the hands of the Confederacy at the start of the Civil War, and the powder in the magazine provided the Confederate troops the much needed ammunition with which to fight during the first year of the conflict. Union forces took control of the arsenal and powder magazine on May 9, 1862, when Admiral Farragut and his men captured it with little resistance at all, the Confederate troops having withdrawn from Baton Rouge. The arsenal and powder magazine would stay under Union control for the remainder of the war.

View of the wall surrounding the powder magazine, which is now the Old Arsenal Museum. *Photo by Hope Steed Kennedy.*

Today, the arsenal has been completely restored and houses the Old Arsenal Museum, which showcases the history of the arsenal and the part it played in the Civil War.

BILLY BOY'S GHOST

I first heard this story over twenty years ago while unloading my semitrailer at a storage warehouse in Baton Rouge. The forklift operator went to lunch while in the middle of unloading the trailer, so I followed him on down to the break room and visited with him and his fellow workers while they had lunch. It was in October, and Halloween was just around the corner, so naturally our conversations turned to memories of trick-or-treating and then to ghost stories we had heard.

One story that was shared with me was that of the ghost called Billy Boy Blue, who supposedly haunted the grounds around the old powder magazine area. How he got the name no one seemed to know, but it was speculated that the "Blue" part was due to his Union uniform.

As the story goes, after General Lee surrendered at Appomattox, Confederate soldiers slowly started to make their way home. Emotions still ran high between the returning soldiers and the Union forces stationed at the Baton Rouge Arsenal, partly due to the Union-supported carpetbaggers who descended on the South like a bunch of locusts. Verbal outbursts among the three groups were common, sometimes coming to blows or, in this case, murder.

A couple ex-Confederate soldiers had come into town to visit with family members and to get supplies when they were accosted by a group of Union soldiers. The Union soldiers started verbally abusing the ex-Confederates, who gave back to the Union soldiers as good as they were getting in the name-calling department. This all resulted in the outnumbered ex-Confederate soldiers taking a pretty hard beating from the Union troops—so bad, in fact, that one of the ex-Confederate soldiers ended up dying, while the other was laid up for quite some time. This, of course, was reported to the commanding officer of the arsenal, who had the cursory investigation performed. The investigation resulted in the Union troops being cleared of all charges. With one dead and the other badly hurt, there was really no one to contest the Union troop's version of what happened.

Tensions escalated, and with family members of the killed and beaten vowing to seek revenge on the Union soldiers who had instigated the altercation, the lives of two Union soldiers for each of the beaten and killed men were the stated price of retribution. Things quieted down for a few weeks, but then one night, the family members acted on their vow. A lone Union soldier was standing guard at the entrance to the powder magazine

Front entrance to the powder magazine, which now houses the Old Arsenal Museum. *Photo by Hope Steed Kennedy.*

area when he was attacked and killed, his throat slit from ear to ear. Another soldier sounded the alarm when he went to relieve the slain soldier and found him dead, turning out the barracks in a search of the grounds for any sign of the killer. None was found, and after the investigation provided no further leads, the soldier was buried. The official verdict was that someone had an axe to grind with that particular soldier and nothing more. It would seem that no one connected the dots that this soldier was one of the group who had beaten the two ex-Confederate soldiers and against whom the family had vowed to seek revenge.

Several weeks later, after things had quieted down and returned to normal around the barracks, another soldier was killed while standing guard outside the powder magazine entrance. Again, his throat was cut, and the relief guard found his body sitting against the brick wall. Sadly though, as the story was told, this particular Union soldier had not taken part in the beating but was merely a replacement guard that night, substituted for the original guard who had received an injury that had him laid up in the infirmary. Said to be a young man of seventeen, the slain soldier had only recently arrived at the post. Supposedly, word that the wrong man had been killed got back to the family members, who decided that enough blood had been spilled and stopped with the revenge killings.

Several months later, the soldier who had been injured and replaced with the young man who was killed started acting strangely, talking to himself and telling everyone, "Billy won't let me be." Apparently, the spirit of the young man who had been killed, young Billy, was tormenting the other soldier, rightfully mad that he had been mistakenly killed in his place. A few weeks later, they found the man hanging from a ceiling beam, driven to suicide by the ghost of Billy.

After that, the spirit of Billy was seen around the powder magazine walking his post as if still on guard duty. Other soldiers who were assigned guard duty at the magazine reported that they were approached by a young soldier who asked if they were his relief. When they said no and asked him who he was, he replied, "Why, Billy of course." Then smiling, he would simply fade away, leaving the soldier dumbfounded as to what he had just seen. He appeared to so many soldiers that the running joke was that anytime something fell or there was an unknown noise, "Billy Boy" was the culprit.

They say that the ghost of Billy is still seen on occasion, walking guard duty in the early morning hours at the powder magazine, apparently still waiting on someone to relieve him.

THE INQUISITIVE GHOST

Another story that I had heard at the same time was about a ghost that wanders around the grounds of the old powder magazine during the day. People have reported being approached by a person in full Civil War military garb who curiously asks questions about who they are and why they are there. The spirit is said to ask questions about personal items that the person is carrying, such as a camera. People assume he is an actor portraying a Union soldier as part of an interpretive program, acting as if he is unfamiliar with modern items. The people play along and even compliment him on staying in character. Understandably, when they part ways and someone looks back only to find that the soldier isn't there any longer, they get a little bewildered. Witnesses have described him as an average-looking young man, well mannered and polite and with a neat and tidy appearance. No one knows who the soldier is, as he has never given a name when asked. Perhaps it's the ghost of Billy Boy Blue making a daytime appearance? I suppose it's as plausible an explanation as any.

CHAPTER 3

BATON ROUGE
NATIONAL CEMETERY

Officially established in 1868 as a burial space for Union soldiers killed in the area, the Baton Rouge National Cemetery had already held the graves of soldiers killed in the Battle of Baton Rouge. It was a short but bloody battle, with the Union forces holding the high ground at the west end of the cemetery and the adjacent Magnolia Cemetery. Confederate General John C. Breckinridge, formerly a United States Vice President, staged the attack to try and reclaim the city for the Confederate forces. At the end of the battle, the losses were fairly even, with the Confederate forces reporting 84 killed, 315 wounded and 57 missing or captured and the Union forces reporting a loss of 84 soldiers killed, 266 wounded and 33 missing or captured. The Union dead were buried where the National Cemetery now sits.

With the establishment of the National Cemetery, it was decreed that Union soldiers who had died in battle, from wounds and from disease who were buried in small graveyards around the area would be reinterred in the new National Cemetery. Later, a large number of additional bodies would be relocated from graveyards at Plaquemine, Louisiana, and Camden, Arkansas. The thought was that it would be easier for their relatives to find and care for the graves if the bodies were moved, identified and placed in one area. Unfortunately, out of the 2,936 graves in the cemetery, 494 soldiers' remains could not be identified and are marked unknown.

While the majority of those buried there are Union soldiers, the cemetery also holds the remains of soldiers who served in the Revolutionary War, the

Entrance gate to the Baton Rouge National Cemetery. *Courtesy Library of Congress, Prints and Photographs Division, HALS LA-5-1.*

Gravestones at the Baton Rouge National Cemetery. *Photo by Hope Steed Kennedy.*

War of 1812 and the Spanish-American War. The cemetery is beautifully maintained and quite a peaceful place—so peaceful in fact, that a few of the "residents" don't want to leave.

SPIRITS IN THE MIST

Fog and mist in the early morning hours is not uncommon in Baton Rouge, due to the Mississippi River being its western boundary. This story was told to me by a gentleman named James, who I met at a small diner early one morning when I was having breakfast. I was having a cup of coffee waiting on my order to come up when I saw him walk in and take a seat at the table next to me. That he was a little shook up was evident by how his hand trembled slightly when he picked up the water glass the waitress set in front of him. I asked him if he was ok, and he said yes but that he had just had the strangest experience—he had seen not one but a group of ghosts. He said, "I know it sounds crazy, but I swear that's what I saw. They even touched me!" I told him that I didn't think it sounded crazy at all and that I had had similar experiences as a paranormal investigator. Well, when he heard that I was a paranormal investigator and didn't think he was crazy, he just let loose with the whole story.

It seems that James liked to walk in the early morning hours at the Baton Rouge National Cemetery, which is open to the public from daylight to dark. A peaceful place that is well maintained, it is ideal for early morning walkers who are out to get a little exercise before the heat and humidity sets in. That is just what James was doing that morning when he had his encounter. He had been in the cemetery only a brief time, enjoying the coolness of the light fog as he walked. He said the fog was thick in spots but that overall you could see pretty well, so he wasn't worried about bumping into anyone. Near the back part of the cemetery, he said he was suddenly aware of sounds coming from all around him—not loud or overwhelming sounds, just soft and faint. He stopped to listen and said he could make out a jangling type of noise coming from up ahead of him. He decided he would walk toward the noise to see if he could see what was causing it, thinking that perhaps the grounds staff was getting an early start. The farther he went, the louder the noise got, and then he started to hear what sounded like men shouting at each other. A bit concerned that he might be walking into some kind of escalating problem, he eased on a bit farther, although with considerably more caution than before. The voices were getting louder and seemed to be closer to him in the fog, and he said he could clearly hear several horses whinnying, which he found to be extremely odd. What would horses be doing in the cemetery in the early morning fog?

As he started to turn around to move away from the sounds, he saw movement start in the fog ahead of him. He froze in place as he saw a horse pulling a cannon, a rider in a Union uniform astride it, emerge fully from the fog and heading right toward him. Behind the cannon, several uniformed men rushed from the fog, and as they drew close to James, they all stopped and stared at him. They saw him, and he saw them—that much was apparent. As he stood there rooted to the spot, the men behind the cannon walked up cautiously to him as if as unsure of what they were seeing. All around him, James could hear voices talking in a low, quiet tone, but he admitted he was concentrating so much on the armed soldiers and the horse in front of him that he paid no attention to what they were saying. One of the soldiers moved up close to James and cautiously, as if afraid of what he was seeing, reached out and touched James's arm and said, "Who are you?" That was all it took for James to suddenly find his feet, and he turned to run as fast as he could away from the group. As he looked over his shoulder as he ran, he saw them slowly dissolve into the fog. He never broke stride all the way to his car and drove away from the cemetery as quickly as he could, trying to fight down the panic and get control of himself. After a few blocks,

Speaker's platform at the Baton Rouge National Cemetery. *Photo by Hope Steed Kennedy.*

he pulled over and just sat there trying to calm down and rationalize what he had just witnessed.

When he regained his composure, he realized that he wanted to go to a more public place with plenty of people around him—sort of a safe haven—and he pulled into the first restaurant that he found.

As we sat there talking over what he had just experienced, I could tell that he was sincere and accurate in his account. It was evident that he was still upset, jumping every time the door from the kitchen slammed shut. I told him that he was incredibly lucky to have witnessed what he did and that I certainly wished that it had been me instead of him who had had the encounter with the Union troops. His only reply was, "I wish it had been you, too."

The Walker

Several years ago, I had a story related to me by an older lady from Baton Rouge who was vacationing in Biloxi, Mississippi, and staying at the same condominium complex that my family and I were staying at. I was coming back up the elevator with her and had on my TOPS (The Ozarks Paranormal Society) shirt when she smiled at me and commented on my shirt, asking if I was "one of those ghost-hunting guys." I told her that I was indeed a paranormal investigator and a writer and that my family and I were vacationing in Biloxi, our favorite spot to go hang out at. She told me that she was taking a weekend holiday herself and was from Baton Rouge. After a bit more meaningless and polite chitchat, she looked at me and said, "I have a story to tell you about the National Cemetery in Baton Rouge if you would like to hear it." I assured her that I would.

She told me that she and a group of her friends would get together almost every morning and power walk in the National Cemetery. From the first day they went there, they noticed an elderly man with a cane walking slowly among the gravestones and markers, and since he was close to where they were walking, they said good morning to him. He failed to acknowledge their greeting and just kept on walking slowly around the graves. A little put off by his rudeness, they nonetheless shrugged it off and continued on their way. Each day after that, they would see him in the same general area, and each day they would say good morning to him. Every day, he would ignore their greeting, walking slowly along among the gravestones as if the women weren't even there. Well, that aggravated the ladies, and they made up their minds that they were going to get him to speak to them or at least acknowledge them in some way—they viewed it as a sort of challenge. This went on for several weeks until finally the ladies decided to confront the old man about his lack of good manners and how he should at least show common civility by greeting them in return. They met the next morning and set out on their walk around the cemetery, and true to form, there was the elderly man with the cane, walking around the same section of graves. They said good morning, and when they got no response, they descended in force upon the old man, ready to give him a lesson in manners that a man of his age should already know. As they approached him, they spoke to him once more, again eliciting no response at all. Clearly aggravated now and summoning up the icy, righteous wrath that every good southern lady who has been rudely ignored can bring forth, they let loose a verbal barrage at him, taking him to task about his rudeness. The old man never even batted an eye; he just kept walking around among the graves as if he didn't even hear or see them. One of the ladies had finally had enough and reached out her hand to take hold of the old man's arm only to see it pass right through him. Shocked, they stood there quietly, rooted to the spot with disbelief and staring at him with open mouths. That's when the old man finally seemed to

Rows of gravestones at the Baton Rouge National Cemetery. *Photo by Hope Steed Kennedy.*

take notice of them, and shaking his cane at them, he said, "Why don't you nosy old bitties just leave me alone? I can't find Ellen with y'all cacklin' at me!" Then he shook his cane at them one more time and faded away right before their eyes. That broke the spell that the women were under, and with a chorus of shrieks, they ran from the cemetery back to their cars. It was several weeks before they met again to walk in the cemetery, and they did so with much trepidation, expecting to see the cranky old ghost again. As they slowly eased up to the spot where they had seen him, they were relieved to see that he wasn't there. They never saw the old man at the cemetery again. Where he went from that point is anyone's guess, but one thing is pretty certain: wherever he went, he just wanted to be left alone to look for Ellen. I, for one, hope he finds her.

CHAPTER 4

USS *KIDD*

S itting in a specially designed dry dock cradle that allows it to float during times of high water, the USS *Kidd* (DD-661) sits as a memorial to the brave men who served aboard it during World War II and the Korean Conflict. The Louisiana Naval War Memorial Commission maintains and operated the Fletcher-class destroyer, the only known destroyer in the world restored to its World War II configuration. The *Kidd* is a military memorial to all who have served their country, and it is solely funded through donations, gift-shop sales, ticket sales and special events, including camping aboard the vessel.

Named after Rear Admiral Isaac C. Kidd, who was killed aboard his ship, the USS *Arizona*, in the surprise attack on Pearl Harbor in 1941, the USS *Kidd* was built and launched from the Federal Shipbuilding and Dry-Dock Company in Kearny, New Jersey, on February 28, 1943. Rear Admiral Kidd's widow spoke with naval brass after being contacted by the crew of the *Kidd* about adopting the infamous Captain William Kidd, an eighteenth-century pirate, as their mascot. She thought it was appropriate since her husband's nickname at the naval academy was "Cap," so permission was received for the USS *Kidd* to fly the Jolly Roger from the mast. The *Kidd* was the only ship in American naval history to be granted permission to fly the pirate flag, and the crew would soon hire an artist to paint an image of Captain Kidd on the smokestack. The ship would be known as the "Pirate of the Pacific."

During wartime, the *Kidd* sailed with a compliment of 330 men and saw action throughout the Atlantic and Pacific theaters. During its participation

View of the USS *Kidd* showing the unique floating cradle system that supports the boat during the fluctuating water levels common on the Mississippi River. *Photo by Hope Steed Kennedy.*

at the Battle of Okinawa, it was struck by a Japanese kamikaze attack that resulted in the deaths of 38 crew members and an additional 55 wounded. There is a page on the *Kidd's* website listing the names of those killed (including biographies for some of them), and I would recommend that everyone take a moment to go to www.usskidd.com and take the time to read about these American heroes and the history of the ship.

The *Kidd* was finally decommissioned on June 19, 1964, after providing over twenty years of service to our country. The *Kidd* was deemed unfit for service in 1975 and struck from the naval list of vessels, but it wasn't destined for the scrap yards like so many others. It was towed from the naval shipyards at Philadelphia and arrived in Baton Rouge May 23, 1982, with over ten thousand people welcoming it to its new home. August 27, 1983 was the date of the *Kidd's* official opening to the public, and the ship has since been restored to its former glory, a suitable monument to the men and women of our armed forces and a reminder of the sacrifice and bravery of those who have willingly placed themselves "in harm's way."

BELOW DECKS

I was told this story just a year ago, shortly after it was purported to have happened, by a gentleman who was part of a group spending the night aboard the *Kidd*. He also happened to be a paranormal investigator, although he was not on board the *Kidd* in that capacity but rather as part of a family reunion of which he and several members of his family decided to forego the hotel room and stay on the ship.

They stowed their gear in their berthing area, went through the fire drill procedure and started off on the guided tour of the ship. The tour was fascinating, and when they came to one of the ammunition handling rooms, the guide explained everything in the room and the procedures that the handlers would have gone through as they passed the ammunition up to the gun crew. He said he didn't see anything at that time but that the feeling of extreme tension and stress suddenly came over him in waves. His heart started racing, and his breathing suddenly became labored, but he was at a loss to explain what was happening or why it was happening. He told me that emotional experiences such as those almost never happened to him and that he really didn't place much faith in them as being paranormal in nature, since he preferred to investigate the paranormal from a scientific perspective and not a metaphysical one. However, he did think to himself that it was an area that bore further examination, and as soon as the free time arrived where they could explore the ship on their own, he and his brother made their way around the ship with the main purpose of examining the ammunition handling room.

As they got close to the handling room, they started to hear little clanking sounds—like those you would hear from tools being used and then set down or knocked against the metal accidentally. As they started to enter the room, they heard a pretty loud "bang," as if something had dropped in the room, and they immediately thought that someone else was in there with them. After looking all around, they couldn't find anyone or anything, so they decided to go over next to the wall by some projectiles, sit down and just remain quiet for a little bit.

The man told me they had been sitting there quietly for about fifteen minutes when they started to hear faint sounds in the room. The sounds of footsteps became quite clear, as if several people were walking around the room right in front of them; however, there was no one present. What followed next were the faint sounds of conversation, as if a discussion among at least three people were taking place, the difference in the voices being plain although the words were not clear. Thinking that perhaps the sounds were simply carrying in from somewhere else on the ship, he got up, leaving his brother still sitting by the wall, and eased out into the passageway to see if he could hear any noise or voices. The sounds continued as he eased out of the room, and as he stood in the passage, it became clear that they were coming from the ammunition handling room he had just left. Thinking that perhaps they were coming from the gun mount directly above the room, he quietly moved back into the room and up to the powder passers platform where the powder canisters were passed up to the gun crew. Standing very still, he listened to the sounds and became convinced that they were not coming from the gun mount but from the very room they were in.

As he stepped away from the platform to go sit back down with his brother, he passed through a huge cold spot—so cold that he could see his breath—and goose bumps came up on his arms. He went on and sat down beside his brother, and quietly they continued to listen to the sounds in front of them. They could clearly hear footsteps and voices in front of them, and they sat there listening intently, trying to make out what was being said. Suddenly, one voice got louder than the others, and both brothers clearly heard the words "below decks." Several times in the next couple of minutes, they heard the same voice saying "below decks" but couldn't make out what else was being said. The footsteps got louder in front of them and suddenly there stood a sailor looking directly at them. I use the word "stood," although my friend said the sailor was missing his legs from about the knees down. Not that they were missing from being blown off or anything like that, they just started to fade out and disappear at the knee. They sat there rooted to the spot staring at the soldier when my friend found his voice and asked the sailor if he could tell them his name. The sailor remained silent and just stood there looking at them. My friend asked the sailor if he could tell them what he wanted, to which the sailor looked at him and said, "You should leave. You're not supposed to be below decks." The sailor then turned and moved out of the door into the passage and faded from sight.

My friend and his brother got up quickly and looked up and down the passage, but no one could be seen. They both went back into the room and stood there for a few moments looking at each other, grinning like a couple of fools at what they had just witnessed. The sounds around them had ceased, so they decided to go on up on deck for a breath of fresh air and discuss what they had just seen.

As they stepped out on deck, my friend's brother jokingly said out loud, "There, are you happy now?" A moment later, they heard a very clear "Yes" come from right behind them, but of course when they turned around, no one was there.

My friend told me that his greatest regret was not having his digital voice recorder or a camera with him, as what he and his brother experienced

Partial front view of the USS *Kidd*. *Photo by Hope Steed Kennedy.*

was a once-in-a-lifetime kind of thing. I asked him what he thought the sailor was doing and why he told them they didn't belong below decks. His take on it was that the sailor was simply continuing to follow orders by keeping visitors to the ship out of what would have been a restricted area. Either way, it turned out to be quite an interesting family reunion sleepover on the USS *Kidd*.

OTHER EXPERIENCES

Other people have reported paranormal experiences on the USS *Kidd* over the years since it first opened to the public in 1983. Sightings of sailors moving through the passageways only to disappear a moment after being seen, spirits fading from sight when someone would enter a room, the sound of phantom footsteps ringing down the decks as if several people were running and the sounds of tapping and knocking on the walls have all been reported over the years. One person reported being woken up in the early morning hours by someone tapping him on the foot as they slept in one of the berthing compartments. Another woke up when she thought she felt someone sit down on the edge of the bunk she was in.

All in all, though, I haven't heard of any accounts in which the person felt threatened—in fact, it's been just the opposite. While being initially startled at what they felt or saw, the feeling passed almost immediately, replaced by a feeling of safety and security. Perhaps the sailors still standing the eternal watch on the USS *Kidd* are simply there out of a sense of duty, keeping an eye on the ship and its passengers.

CHAPTER 5

HIGHLAND ROAD

One of the most recurring reports of spirit sightings in the Baton Rouge area happens in the Highland Road area around the end of September through October. Beginning on Highland Road near Lee Drive and continuing down to Gardere Lane, numerous people have reported seeing Confederate soldiers walking along the roadway or running across it. The sightings do not seem to adhere to any particular time of day or even day of the week, as reports have placed them on or crossing the roadway at all times.

One story that I heard about but have not been able to confirm happened in October 1999 at about 5:00 p.m., right as people were on their way home from work. Supposedly, several people called the police to report a man who appeared to be injured and bleeding, dressed in a dirty Confederate uniform and carrying a rifle. He paused at the side of the road for a few moments as if to catch his breath and then staggered on across the road, collapsing to his hands and knees for a few moments before struggling to his feet and moving away.

The several drivers who reported the occurrence stopped and witnessed the whole thing; one of them even got out of his car and rushed after the soldier but could not find him. When the police arrived on scene, the witnesses directed them to where the soldier had disappeared, but a search of the area revealed nothing at all.

Another sighting in September 2001 was witnessed by a family of five who were on their way home after having watched a movie. They had just passed Lee Drive when a group of Confederate soldiers suddenly showed

Planters Cabin on Highland Road. *Courtesy Library of Congress, Prints and Photographs Division, HABS LA, 17-BATRO, 9-14 (ct).*

up in their headlights. The soldiers were walking down the side of the road, two of them supporting what appeared to be an injured comrade. When the family drew abreast of the group, one of the soldiers turned and stepped out slightly into the roadway, raising his weapon as if to protect the group should it become necessary. The wife, who was in the passenger seat, immediately called the police to report a group of armed men, one of whom appeared to be hurt, walking down the side of Highland Road. Again, a search of the area turned up absolutely zilch, but everyone in the family agreed on what had been seen. Both of the parents commented on how haggard, dirty and just plain worn out the men looked, their uniforms torn and stained—the kids just thought it was cool, though.

At the beginning of October 2003, a man and his wife were going to dinner and were driving down Highland Road. As in the previous story, just past Lee Drive, they saw a group of what appeared to be Confederate soldiers walking down the side of the road. As they neared the group, the soldiers suddenly darted across the road, running right out in front of them. The man hit his brakes hard and swerved to the right but didn't quite clear the last soldier, striking him with the left front of his pickup truck. The sound of impact was clearly audible to the couple. Coming to a stop, the man leaped from his truck and ran back toward where the fallen man should have been; however, there was no one to be found. While the man searched both sides of the road, his wife called the police to report the accident, but try as he might, the man could find no one. Walking back to his truck, he looked at the front where he had hit the soldier to see what kind of damage there was. Curiously, there wasn't a scratch, dent or even a broken headlight—there was no sign of impact at all. Both of them clearly heard and felt the impact between the soldier and the front of the pickup truck and were at a loss to explain why there was no damage. When officers arrived on scene, the area was searched, but once again, no one could be found.

Why these sightings keep happening toward the end of September through October is unknown, but perhaps the soldiers are falling back from some skirmish or another. One thing is for certain, however, and that is that numerous people have seen Confederate soldiers crossing or walking beside the road many times—too many times to be mere coincidence or fabricated stories, in my opinion.

CHAPTER 6

THE OLD STATE CAPITOL BUILDING

O n September 21, 1847, the City of Baton Rouge donated a parcel of land to the State of Louisiana for the purpose of building a new state capitol. This would cause the state capitol to be moved from New Orleans to a bluff facing the Mississippi River where some believed that the original site of "Le Baton Rouge," or the Red Stick, that the French explorers named the area for was located.

Designed by James Harrison Dakin, a successful architect from New Orleans, the building was crafted to give the appearance of a fifteenth-century Gothic castle, or as Dakin referred to it, a "Castellated Gothic." Sporting a floor plan complete with towers, stained-glass windows, gables and extensive cast-iron decorations, the building is very unusual and distinctive, garnering initial ridicule from numerous individuals, including Mark Twain. However, it is one of the best examples of Gothic Revival architecture in the United States.

The building was finished in 1852 and served as the seat of Louisiana's government until 1862, when Union Admiral David Farragut captured Baton Rouge. The statehouse was then pressed into service as a Union prison and later as a garrison for African American troops under the command of General Culver Grover. The building caught fire twice while being used as

Next page, top: Older photo of the Old State Capitol Building. *Courtesy Library of Congress, Prints and Photographs Division, HABS LA, 17-BATRO, 6-1.*

Next page, bottom: Interior staircase at the Old State Capitol Building. *Courtesy Library of Congress, Prints and Photographs Division, HABS LA, 17-BATRO, 6-13.*

a garrison, and the fire-gutted shell was abandoned by Union troops a short time later.

By 1882, the ruined interior was completely restored by engineer and architect William A. Freret, who was responsible for installing the grand staircase and the beautiful stained-glass dome. It would remain the statehouse until 1932, when the new state capitol was finished and the legislature officially transferred the seat of government for Louisiana to the newly finished building. In 1936, the Works Progress Administration began using the old building as its headquarters, but by the late 1980s, the building had fallen into a state of neglect and looked as if it was destined for demolition. In 1991, a group of citizens and politicians rallied to save the old capitol, and a huge restoration project began to bring the building back to its former glory. Today, the Old State Capitol building is a National Historic Landmark and home to the Center for Political and Government History.

PIERRE COUVILLION

One of the best-known tales of the Old State Capitol building is that of Legislator Pierre Couvillion, a representative of Avoyelles Parish who reportedly died in the building in 1852 during a heated debate over gambling. He was the victim of a heart attack at age forty-seven. While he is said to be buried close to his home, near Marksville, it is thought that his spirit still roams the halls and rooms of the old statehouse where he died. Several people have encountered what they believe to be the spirit of Couvillion in the upstairs hallways, and security guards have watched while motion detectors went off as if someone was walking down the hallway but of course no one was visible on the monitors.

One of the stories about an encounter with the ghost of Pierre Couvillion was shared with me by a former security officer (we will call him "Tom" since he asked me not to use his real name in the story), who also related several other stories to me about unexplained events that were witnessed in other parts of the building, most specifically the basement area.

Tom was working the late shift at the Old State Capitol building and hadn't been employed there very long when he had his first encounter. He had been told by various co-workers that the building was haunted, but at the time, he really didn't place much faith in the prospect of ghosts being real. He had always believed that there was a logical explanation for everything.

Tom had just embarked on his walking patrol, checking doors and windows and making sure that everything was secure on the bottom floor, and proceeded to climb the grand staircase to check out the second floor. As he paused at the top of the staircase, he heard a slight tapping sound coming from down the hallway, just a soft tap...tap…tap. Thinking that a fan or air-conditioning vent was blowing on something and causing it to make the noise, he simply disregarded it and started on down the hallway, checking rooms as he went. He was about halfway down the hallway when he noticed that the tapping noise was getting louder and louder and coming more quickly, and it sounded as if it was coming from directly in front of him although there was obviously nothing there. Curious as to what was causing the noise, he abandoned his check of the rooms and moved ahead to where the sound seemed to be coming from: directly ahead of him and in the middle of the hallway. As he moved ahead and into the center of the hall, the noise got continually louder and faster—TAP TAP TAP TAP—and he admitted to me that at this point, he was starting to get a little jumpy. But his curiosity drove him forward, determined to find the logical explanation for the noise and to ensure that it wasn't anything that might be causing damage to the building. He had moved forward about another ten feet when he suddenly became very aware of a drop in temperature, the air becoming cold enough to raise goose bumps on his arms. Thinking that perhaps the problem lay within the air-conditioning system, he started to pay closer attention to the cold, holding his hand out in front of himself and trying to find a draft or air flow that might lead him to the source of the sudden temperature drop. The air was completely still, but the chill continued. Admittedly perplexed by what he was experiencing, at the time, he didn't equate it to anything that might be paranormal in nature.

He was about to drop his hand back down to his side when, all of a sudden, he felt what he described as a light slap on the back of his hand. Startled, he jerked his hand back and involuntarily took a step backward only to bump into someone behind him. Thinking that perhaps a fellow security officer had slipped up behind him, he spun around only to come face to face with who he believes was Pierre Couvillion. He described the figure as a middle-aged man with "salt-and-pepper" hair, bushy side burns and a thin mustache and dressed in an old-fashioned suit. But what was most remarkable was that the man appeared to give off a slight glow. As Tom stood there staring open mouthed at the figure before him, unable to comprehend what he was seeing, the figure before him made a simple step to the side and said "Pardon me" in a French accent as he slightly nodded his head and then moved past him at a leisurely pace. Stunned, Tom turned to watch the man stroll on down the hallway and turn into a room at the end of it.

Suddenly realizing that an unauthorized stranger, not to mention one who appeared out of nowhere and who was dressed in old-fashioned clothes, had just walked past him, Tom rushed down to the end of the hallway and burst into the room the figure had just entered. Flipping on the light switch, he quickly scanned the room. Seeing no one there, he searched the entire area, even under the two desks and in the supply cabinet, but he could find no one. With only one way in and one way out, Tom was completely stumped as to where the person had gone—they seemed to have disappeared into thin air!

Tom then radioed to the security desk and asked his counterpart if he had just seen what had happened and if he had seen the man emerge from any other room. The guard at the desk simply replied that he hadn't seen any man or anything other than Tom spin around in the hallway and then rush down to the end of the hall and disappear into the room that he was now standing in the doorway of. Completely bewildered at what had happened, Tom immediately returned to the security desk and asked the other guard once more if he had seen anything at all in the hallway, to which he received the same reply: nothing at all. A quick review of the security tape from that camera also revealed nothing other than Tom and his strange reaction to something unseen.

The Old State Capitol Building as it looks today. *Photo by Hope Steed Kennedy.*

After Tom related his story to the other guard, the man simply chuckled and shook his head, saying, "You must have seen ol' Pierre. He's supposed to haunt this place." To this day, Tom still doesn't have a logical explanation for what happened, although he did have this to say about it:

> *I have never been one to believe in ghosts and such. I always thought that they were just silly stories made up to scare little kids or torment grown men who were afraid of their own shadows. But after seeing what I did, I can't help but believe now that maybe there might be such a thing as ghosts. I mean really, where did the guy who walked into the room go? Not past me, that's for sure! And why didn't he show up on the security tape? Maybe it was the ghost of Pierre Couvillion—I tend to think that it was. I really don't know what else to think.*

THE SOLDIER

The basement of the Old State Capitol building seems to be home to the ghost of a Civil War soldier—maybe even more than one.

During the Union occupation of Baton Rouge, the Old State Capitol building was pressed into service as a Union hospital, garrison and jail. The upper floors were being used as the garrison (barracks), while the basement was being used as the hospital, surgery room and jail.

When the building was going through one of its renovations, a brick wall in the basement was accidentally opened up, revealing a jail cell complete with Civil War–era artifacts. It is believed that the cell was bricked off some time close to the end of the war, although no one seems to know the reason why.

A new door, resembling a solid type of jail cell door with viewing slits, one at eye level for an adult and another at eye level for a child, was put in place to keep people out of the jail area, and it was left pretty much as it was found, artifacts and all. However, an interesting addition to the jail cell is that of the projection of a Civil War–era inmate sitting on the bunk who fades in and out of sight. A plaque near the doorway reads:

> *This mysterious jail cell was discovered when a brick wall was accidentally demolished during recent renovations. The cell is believed to have been used by the office of Provost Marshal, which was the law enforcement arm of the occupying Union army during the Civil War. In 1862, the Provost*

Marshal used the State House as headquarters and used some parts of the building to hold prisoners for civil offenses and anti-Union activities.

The cell remains exactly as it was found. The objects have been identified as authentic to the Civil War era, but little is known beyond that. Since the discovery of this lost cell, some people claim to have experienced unexplainable, ghostly things down here. While no one has been able to confirm this strange phenomenon, you may want to judge for yourself. Take a look.

Perhaps the last part of the plaque simply implants the idea into people's minds that the area is haunted, but numerous people have experienced what they described as the ghost of a Union soldier walking throughout the area shortly after the discovery of the jail cell.

Tom, the security officer who related to me the story of Pierre Couvillion, also told me of an encounter he had with the ghost of a Union soldier while doing his rounds one night. He had just descended the stairs to the basement area and was walking along checking rooms as he headed down to check the outside door. As he passed the room that was reported to have been used as the surgery room during the Union occupation, he heard what sounded like a tool being dropped on the floor. Thinking that someone was in the room, he immediately stepped inside and flipped on the lights. What he saw, however, wasn't an intruder but rather the figure of a Union soldier walking around the room. He called out to the figure, telling him to halt, but the man just kept on walking about the room as if performing some series of tasks.

As Tom moved farther into the room, the figure of the soldier continued to ignore him, and as if he had completed his task, he turned and walked right past him and out into the hallway. A completely bewildered Tom followed him out into the hallway and watched him walk down to the entrance to the jail cell area and turn into it. He rushed down to the entrance and cautiously peered around the corner toward the slotted jail door, but there was no one to be seen. Doubting what he had just seen, a now-jittery Tom walked back out into the hallway and started toward the outside door to check and make sure it was secure. He hadn't walked but a few steps when he heard what sounded like two men talking behind him, so he quickly turned around, although he admitted he was a bit worried about what he might see. As he stood there, he saw the figure of the same soldier walk back out of the jail cell area, talking as if someone was beside him. The man walked back toward the surgery room, continuing his conversation with his unseen companion, and simply disappeared right there in the hallway.

Oddly, the sounds of their conversation continued for a few moments after the soldier had disappeared.

Thoroughly creeped out, Tom made a hasty retreat from the basement, foregoing any other investigation as to what might have happened or who the soldier might have been. He recalled, "At that point, I could care less about who they were, what they were doing or why they were in that basement. I just knew I wasn't going to hang out down there any longer than I had to. They could have that basement all to themselves as far as I was concerned. I wasn't having any part of it."

I asked Tom if he could describe what the man looked like. He said the man was rather young in age, maybe in his mid-twenties, and that he was cleanshaven with brown, wavy hair. He was of average height and walked with an odd gait, as if he was slightly lame. He was also dressed in what appeared to be a Union uniform, although he wore no coat and his shirt sleeves were rolled up as if he had been at work at some messy task. He looked for all the world as if he was a solid, living, breathing person who was simply going about his job.

Tom said that he never saw the man again, although he would hear him talking from time to time when he would go back down to the basement on his rounds. The conversation was always the same and seemed to be the soldier talking to another person about a lack of supplies.

With the lack of interaction and the same conversation being heard each time, one can only wonder if this might not be a residual haunting—an imprint from a time past left to replay itself as if it were a video on loop.

OTHER EXPERIENCES

Other people have experienced things in the Old State Capitol building from time to time, including everything from hearing whispered voices that seemed to be right next to the persons ear to being touched or poked or having one's hair pulled. Other people have seen the figure of a woman in period clothing walking down the hallways and stairs from time to time as well. She appears to be very friendly, and the feeling experienced by those who have seen her was one of warmth and protectiveness. It is thought that she is the spirit of Sarah Morgan, whose family is reported to have donated the land that the building sits upon.

A little research into Sarah Morgan revealed that she had spent some time at the Old State Capitol building both before the war and during the

Union occupation of Baton Rouge. Her diaries were published in 1913 under the title *A Confederate Girls Diary, by Sarah Morgan Dawson* (she eventually married Captain Francis Warrington Dawson, an English volunteer in the Confederate navy) and provide an interesting glimpse into life in Baton Rouge during the Civil War years. She mentions attending functions and visiting with other residents at the Old State Capitol building, so it's obvious that the building played an important part in her life as well as playing an important part in the community as a gathering place not only for legal business but also social encounters. She also mentions in her July 29, 1863 entry of seeing first-hand the sick, wounded and dying being discharged from boats arriving at Baton Rouge and how they were scattered all about awaiting transport to the hospital facilities:

This town, with its ten thousand soldiers, is more quiet than it was with the old population of seven thousand citizens. With this tremendous addition, it is like a graveyard in its quiet, at times. These poor soldiers are dying awfully. Thirteen went yesterday. On Sunday, the boats discharged hundreds of sick at our landing. Some lay there all the afternoon in the hot sun, waiting for the wagon to carry them to the hospital, which task occupied the whole evening. In the mean time, these poor wretches lay uncovered on the ground, in every stage of sickness. Cousin Will saw one lying dead without a creature by to notice when he died. Another was dying and muttering to himself as he lay too far gone to brush the flies out of his eyes and mouth, while no one was able to do it for him. Cousin Will helped him, though. Another, a mere skeleton, lay in the agonies of death, too; but he evidently had kind friends, for several were gathered around holding him up and fanning him while his son leaned over him crying aloud. Tiche says it was dreadful to hear the poor boy's sobs. All day our vis-à-vis, Baumstark, with his several aids, plies his hammer; all day Sunday he made coffins, and he says he can't make them fast enough. Think, too, he is by no means the only undertaker here! Oh, I wish these poor men were safe in their own land! It is heartbreaking to see them die here like dogs with no one to say Godspeed. The Catholic priest went to see some, sometime ago, and going near one who lay in bed, said some kind thing, when the man burst into tears and cried, "Thank God, I have heard one kind word before I die!" In a few minutes, the poor wretch was dead.

That she could express compassion for those suffering enemy soldiers gives testament to the good and kind heart that she must have possessed and

Coaling Admiral Farragut's fleet at Baton Rouge during the Civil War. *Courtesy Library of Congress, Prints and Photographs Division, LC-DIG-PPMSCA-10906.*

affirms the feelings that those who have seen what is believed to be her spirit at the Old State Capitol building as being true.

The University of North Carolina at Chapel Hill has scanned the diaries of Sarah Morgan and made them available online for all to read. I would recommend that anyone interested in the Civil War and life in Baton Rouge during that time would be well served to visit the website listed in the bibliography of this book and read the diaries, as they provide valuable first-hand insight into the death and suffering that occurred in and around Baton Rouge and shed light on why the area could be as haunted as it is.

All in all, the Old State Capitol building is a beautifully restored building, its walls and grounds having borne witness to much history over the years. Should it still have a ghost or two remaining within its walls simply lends credence to the esteem with which the old statehouse is held by those who walked its halls.

CHAPTER 7

THE OLD BATON ROUGE GENERAL HOSPITAL

Located at 929 Government Street, the old Baton Rouge General Hospital, now known as the Guaranty Income Life and Broadcasting Building, looks like any other large office building downtown, bustling with activity and the comings and goings of both employees and visitors. Built in the 1920s, it was once a state-of-the-art medical facility but is now home to the Guaranty Corporation, a company with five broadcasting stations in Baton Rouge and an insurance company licensed in thirty-one states.

During the remodeling process after the Guaranty Corporation had taken possession of the old hospital facility, the morgue, which was located in the basement of the building, was converted to a file storage facility. A cafeteria, storage and additional offices were also located in the basement area of the building. Over the years, the building has been home to several other businesses outside of the Guaranty Corporation umbrella, including a doctor's office, a graphic design company and a CPA firm.

Most hospitals, nursing homes and mental health facilities across the nation (and across the world, for that matter) have some story related to a spirit or other paranormal experience, so it seems only logical that the Guaranty Income Life and Broadcasting Building would have its share of stories, too. It also seems logical that facilities that deal in tragedy and death would have some type of paranormal happenings, whether intelligent hauntings or merely the residual imprint of some emotional trauma. That said, some of the experiences that people have had while in the building overnight lend themselves well to what one might expect from a former medical facility. A lot of people who

The old Baton Rouge General Hospital, now known as the Guaranty Income Life and Broadcasting Building. *Photo by Hope Steed Kennedy.*

have worked in the building during the evening and overnight hours have experienced something unexplainable, whether that be disembodied voices, a reflection in a mirror or window of someone who wasn't there or an encounter with the alleged spirit of a former patient or staff member. The question lingers, though, as to just why a spirit would remain in a place to which it had no known emotional attachment. Certainly the spirit of a doctor or a nurse could be explained as remaining due to a sense of caring and a sense of satisfaction related to their job, but why would the spirit of a patient remain? Why would someone stay at a place that held no joyful memories for them but rather memories of pain and death? While we might not have the answers to those types of questions, the fact still remains that something unexplainable is going at the old Baton Rouge General Hospital.

THE ANGRY NURSE

Situated in the basement of the building, the old morgue area now houses a cafeteria, several offices and a storage facility for the cafeteria. The old morgue cooler, once tasked with storing bodies awaiting autopsies or those waiting to be released to family or funeral facilities, now stores only files and records for the Guaranty Corporation. Numerous people who have worked in the basement area have reported strange happenings such as severe temperature drops, unexplainable noises and voices and at least one encounter with a spirit that doesn't really seem all that happy with people invading what she obviously seems to regard as her space.

The story of what I have come to call the "Angry Nurse" was told to me by a lady who once worked in the cafeteria. She was a supervisor of sorts and was responsible for doing some of the office work as well as checking in and receiving supplies for the cafeteria. She would come in early and stay late as necessitated by the job. Anyone who has ever worked in the food-service industry, especially in the kitchen area, knows what a hard and demanding job it can be. Long hours and a fast pace can make for a long day, and it was no different for those working in the cafeteria in the basement of the Guaranty Income Life Building—prep work, cooking, serving and then cleanup, only to get ready to do it all over again for the next meal period.

This woman, who we'll call Cheryl (those of you who have read my other books know that I always change the names of the people who have told me their stories, simply out of respect for their privacy), was working late after everyone had left for the evening, catching up on paperwork and writing up orders for stock that needed to be replenished. She was pecking away at the computer, typing up her order, when she heard what sounded like someone walking around in the kitchen area. Thinking it was most likely a security guard passing through or a member of the kitchen staff returning for some forgotten item, she blew it off and went back to her work. A few more moments passed, and she noticed that the sounds were still carrying on out in the kitchen area, only they were getting louder and starting to sound more like pans and utensils being knocked about than someone walking. Now curious as to whom it might be, she got up from her desk and walked out to the kitchen to see who was responsible for all of the racket. A quick glance showed no one within sight, although the sounds continued to be clearly audible. Confused and more than just a little nervous, she advanced toward the sounds, noticing that some of the pots that were hanging from a rack were starting to swing back and forth, banging into each other slightly. Thinking that it must be something simple like an air vent blowing toward the pans, she relaxed a bit and kind of chuckled to herself about being too jumpy.

Shaking her head, she turned around and almost ran into an elderly lady who was standing right behind her. She let out a little shriek, startled at the sight of the lady and the fact that she had snuck up on her without a sound, and almost involuntarily threw her hands up in front of her as if to keep the lady at arm's length. After a few seconds of gaining her composure, she noticed that the elderly lady was dressed in what appeared to be an all-white old-fashioned nurse's uniform, complete with a cap. She also noticed that the older lady was staring at her with what could only be described as malice; the look of complete hatred and anger that emanated from the old nurse was nearly palpable in its force. Now frightened, Cheryl started to back away from the nurse and stammered out, "Who are you and what do you want?" But she received no answer at all; the old nurse just stood there shooting daggers at Cheryl from her eyes.

Cheryl edged around a worktable and quickly turned to dart to the other end, trying to keep the table between her and the old nurse. As she turned, she was shocked to see the old nurse standing there, still giving her that mean stare. Completely freaked out now, Cheryl backed away quickly, never taking her eyes off the nurse, and asked once more who she was and what she wanted. The mean-eyed old nurse never said a word and just continued staring at Cheryl. Suddenly it seemed as if every pan that was hanging from a hook started to swing wildly back and forth, banging and clanging into each other, louder and louder. Cheryl screamed at the old nurse, "Leave me alone!" and a few seconds later, it was over. It stopped just as suddenly as it had started.

Almost to the point of hysteria, Cheryl turned and ran from the kitchen area back to her office, where she slammed the door, slid a chair under the handle and retreated into the interior of the room just as far as she could go. She told me that after she had fought down the panic and gotten herself a little under control, she realized how foolish shoving the chair under the door handle was, as anything that could suddenly appear and disappear wasn't going to be stopped by a chair under the door handle. After a little while, she grabbed her purse and slowly cracked the door, peeking around it as if afraid of what she might see, but much to her relief, she saw nothing but empty space between her and the exit door. As fast as she could, she bolted across the room and out the exit, never looking back until she reached the relative safety of her car. She kept telling herself as she drove home that she couldn't really have seen what she thought she had seen—it just wasn't possible. Nonetheless, she knew deep down that it had been very real—not a hallucination or an overactive imagination, but a real and extremely terrifying experience.

Cheryl continued working there for a few more weeks but never again stayed in the building by herself. She said that even with a busy kitchen and lots of people around, she just couldn't feel safe anymore, and she would nearly jump out of her skin at the sound of a pan being dropped or accidentally banged into something. To say that her nerves were raw and on edge would be a gross understatement. Finally, she simply couldn't take it anymore and quit, preferring to leave her steady job and deal with being unemployed rather than spend another hour in the basement.

I asked Cheryl if she had ever returned to the basement to see if her feelings of apprehension and fright had lapsed any at all. Without hesitating, she gave an unequivocal and resounding "No!" She admitted that she had thought about it once or twice but that the terrified feelings that she experienced that evening would come rushing back and she would completely put the idea from her mind. No, she is completely fine with leaving well enough alone.

Whether or not the angry old nurse is still hanging out in the basement of the Guaranty Income Life and Broadcasting Building is anyone's guess, as is why she chose to appear to Cheryl that night. Why she was upset and so hateful is a mystery as well. Maybe she was just mad about not having the area to herself that evening and decided to make her feelings known. Either way, she got her point across as far as Cheryl was concerned.

THE DOCTOR

This story was related to me by a young lady named Gwen who worked on the second floor of the building as a secretary. Most days, she would be done by 5:00 p.m., but upon occasion she would have to stay late to finish up the day's work. She said that she had never felt uncomfortable in the building after hours, as there was always security, support staff and other late-night workers, so she was taken by surprise when she encountered the doctor.

Gwen was finishing up typing a report on her computer when she became aware of the feeling of being watched—not a creepy feeling or anything, just that feeling you get when you know someone is watching you and you look up and there they are. Only this time, when she looked up, there wasn't a soul in sight. Shrugging it off, she went back to her computer, but the feeling of being watched persisted. Finally, annoyed at the feeling of being watched, she got up from her desk and walked about the room and even looked out into the hallway, trying to catch someone lurking about spying on her, but still no one was to be seen. She said she had just turned around to walk back to her desk when she caught the figure of someone out of the corner of her eye, and when she turned around, there stood a man in what she described as a white lab coat. He was an older fellow, with thinning hair and glasses that slid down almost to the end of his nose, and he was looking over the top of the glasses right at her. She later said that he reminded her a bit of her grandfather.

Startled, Gwen let out a little gasp and almost involuntarily took a step back. When she regained her composure, she asked him who he was and what he was doing there. She said he smiled at her and let out a little chuckle and said, "Why, I work here, of course." She walked a few steps closer to him, more curious than alarmed, and noticed that he seemed to be completely relaxed. She said you could almost feel the calmness emanating from him, the smile never leaving his face. She asked him again who he was, to which he replied, "I'm just a doctor who works here. Who I am is not important at all, but you, my dear—you look as if you're ill. Are you feeling all right?"

The question struck her as slightly odd, as she was feeling just fine. She told him as much and again asked who he was and what he was doing there. Never losing his smile, the doctor simply told her, "Gwen, you should really see your physician as soon as you can. I've noticed over the last several weeks that you seem to suffer from intense headaches, not migraines, as you tell everyone they are, as from watching you it seems to be localized at the base of your skull, and there doesn't seem to be any sensitivity to light at all. Take my advice, young lady, and see your physician."

Alarmed now, having picked up immediately on the fact that he had been watching her for several weeks and that he had called her by her first name, Gwen turned and reached for the nearest phone to call security, but when she turned back around, he was gone. Security turned out the building, but no one matching the man's description was found in the building. A little concerned, she brushed the whole thing off, noting that she never felt nervous or scared around him.

Several days later, Gwen was at work when she got another severe headache, once again emanating from the base of her skull, only this time it seemed to be just a trifle worse than the last time. The memory of what the mysterious old doctor had told her was still very clear in her mind, so she called and made an appointment to see her doctor to determine the cause of the headaches. After several examinations, including a CAT scan, it was discovered that she had a small tumor located near her spine at the base of her skull. The prognosis wasn't good, and she was told that her survival rate was less than 50 percent but that she was lucky she had come in to get checked out when she did, as any delay in diagnosis and treatment would have significantly lessened her chances of being cured. After several operations and other types of therapy designed to eradicate the tumor, she was pronounced healthy again.

Gwen told me that if she hadn't encountered the doctor that night, she probably wouldn't be alive today, as she would most likely not have sought out medical help until it was too late. As far as she is concerned, the encounter without a doubt saved her life. Just why the doctor appeared to her that night or why he had been paying attention to her over the preceding several weeks is a mystery; maybe she reminded him of someone or perhaps he couldn't stand the thought of not giving her a little nudge toward getting checked out. Whatever the case might be, it was his actions that planted the seed in her mind about getting medical help.

Gwen continued to work in the building for another three years but resigned when she found out she was pregnant, preferring to be a stay-at-home mom rather than a clerical worker. She never saw the doctor again, although she would at times feel as if she were being watched. When she would get those feelings of being watched, she would simply smile and say "thank you" very softly under her breath, knowing that if she hadn't gone looking for the reason behind those feelings, she might not be alive today.

While the paranormal might have its fair share of scary ghosts and unexplainable happenings, every once in a while, it seems the spirits are kind, caring souls that simply want to help.

CHAPTER 8
THE OLD STATE PRISON STORE

In 1832, the Louisiana State Legislature passed a bill for the construction of a state prison to be located in Baton Rouge. By August of that same year, about eight acres were purchased from two individuals, a Mr. John Buhler and a Mr. Raphael Legendre, for the purpose of building the prison. A short time later, one hundred convicts, under sentence of hard labor, were transferred from New Orleans to begin the construction. A warden, ten guards and support personnel were also sent with the prisoners to guard them and manage their work. The total cost of the project was estimated to be $73,000, and a significant amount of money was saved during the construction through the use of the prisoner's labor.

In 1834, it was decided that a storehouse and quarters for the clerks should be added to the complex, and it is around this particular building that many of the stories of ghosts have originated. While I wasn't able to find any historical records of deaths in the prison store itself, there were numerous deaths in the prison complex, and not all of them were state-sanctioned executions. Prison life in the 1800s and early to mid-1900s in Louisiana was no cakewalk, with a lot of the prisoners being leased out to private businesses and farms as cheap disposable labor (one form of slavery was simply traded for another, it would appear). It's estimated that between 1870 and 1901, about three thousand prisoners died from being overworked while leased out by the private company that was in charge of managing the prison facilities for the state. And while the work conditions were horrible, the living conditions weren't much better, with the average prison cell measuring seven

The warden's house and old state prison store. *Courtesy Library of Congress, Prints and Photographs Division, HABS LA, 17-BATRO, 15-16 (ct).*

feet by three and a half feet in diameter. An iron door of approximately twelve inches opened to the cell, which often had no bed and provided little to no heat or ventilation. To survive your sentence in those conditions was testament alone to the toughness of a man.

During the Civil War, the prison was closed and the prisoners were transferred back to New Orleans. The Union army, specifically the Seventh Vermont Regiment, took control and utilized the complex as barracks and headquarters until a fire broke out, causing quite a lot of damage. Little was done to repair the buildings during and immediately after the war, although several hundred prisoners were eventually moved back in by 1868.

The prison itself was operated until about 1917, its last few years being used only as a station to receive new prisoners, an infirmary and an execution facility. The main prison had been moved to Angola, where it remains today.

The prison store building saw many uses over the years, even being used as the home for the prison warden and his family. And it is from that usage that it is also commonly referred to as the Wardens House, being added as such to the National Register of Historic Places in 1974.

THE CONVICT

An interesting story that I heard while visiting Baton Rouge was that of the "Convict," and it had to do with the ghost of a prisoner who seems to haunt the old prison store building. When the building was restored around 1966, it seemed to also restore the ghost of one of the prisoners as well as that of one of the clerks.

The bottom floor of the building was the prison store, where products made by prisoner labor were sold to the public, the proceeds being divided up between the private company that managed the prison and the State of Louisiana. The second floor was divided into living quarters for the clerks who operated the store.

During renovation of the building, one of the workers, Mark, who was assigned the task of stripping out all of the remaining lath and plaster from the walls, was busy on the bottom floor cleaning up a pile of the plaster that he had just torn down. It was pretty hot inside the building, so in the attempt to get some air circulating inside, all of the doors and windows had been opened. When Mark heard someone behind him say, "I do that for you, boss," he assumed that someone had wandered in off the street and was looking for some work. He straightened up and turned around expecting to see the would-be worker standing there, but what he saw was an unkempt young man dressed in dirty, ragged clothes, looking for all the world like a character straight out of a 1930s movie about hobos. Mark was clearly perplexed. He looked at the young man and asked him who he was and what exactly it was that he wanted. The young man simply replied, "I do that for you boss" and shuffled a few steps closer toward Mark, keeping his eyes lowered toward the floor. More curious than alarmed, Mark (who stands six feet, three inches tall and weighed in at 245 pounds when the occurrence happened) leaned on his broom and told the young man that they weren't hiring at the moment and inquired as to just where the young man had come from. The young man stated that he had been sent up from the yard with a new stock of rope for the storehouse and asked where the boss would like him to put it.

More than a little bewildered, Mark looked a little closer at the man standing there and noticed that the shoes he was wearing were made from rough-looking leather, that his pants were torn and ill fitting and that the shirt he wore was a rough pullover that was every bit as dirty as the pants; all in all, he was a pretty sorry-looking character, but he didn't really look to be dangerous. The whole time Mark was looking him over, the young man stood there quietly staring at the floor, his hands folded together and hanging loosely in front of him.

Thinking that the man must be experiencing some kind of mental challenge from the statement about the rope, especially since he wasn't holding any rope, Mark just looked at him and said, "Toss the rope in the corner over there." To his amazement, the young man turned and walked to the corner of the room and went through the motions of dropping something, and then he just stood there quietly in the corner as if waiting for his next orders. Convinced now that the man was obviously mentally challenged, Mark walked over to him and said, "Why don't you come on along with me" and reached out to take him by the arm. As his hand started to close around the young man's upper arm, the man finally looked up at Mark, empty black holes where his eyes should have been.

Mark said he froze right on the spot in complete disbelief. As he stood there, his arm outstretched and his hand almost touching the young man's arm, he suddenly recoiled and literally jumped two feet back. He said the unkempt young man never moved a muscle; he just stared straight ahead at Mark with two empty eye sockets, not saying a word at all. Mark managed to gasp out, "Who the hell are you?!" to which the young man simply replied, "No one any more." And then to the complete horror of Mark, he simply faded away, leaving nothing but a sudden drop in temperature and a wisp of smoke to mark his passing.

It took a moment for Mark to comprehend what he had just seen, and while it's plain to see from just looking at the man that he doesn't scare easy, in this particular instance, Mark nearly tore half the wall down getting out of that room. He said it took him a good thirty minutes before he would go back in the building, easing his way in a bit at a time. He spent the next several days constantly looking over his shoulder while he worked.

The ghost of the convict wasn't the only spirit aroused when the renovations started. What is believed to be the ghost of one of the clerks was spotted briefly on the second floor, although he was heard moving about more frequently. Another man who worked with Mark was on the second floor, doing basically the same thing that Mark was doing on the first floor when he had his encounter, that being cleaning up a mess of fallen and torn-down lath and plaster from the floor. He had stopped for a moment and was leaning on his shovel next to an inside wall that was really nothing more than open studs when he saw a man in old-time clothing walk right past him. Staring in disbelief, he watched as the man passed right through the open wall, walked a few feet into the next room and appeared to take a seat at a table or desk. The man then went through the motions of turning pages and writing something, oblivious to the now-scared man leaning on the shovel. Before the worker could move a muscle, the seated figure called out for someone named Henry and then disappeared. The worker immediately dropped the shovel and exited the building as quickly as he could, not stopping until he made it to his pickup truck. Unlike Mark, this fellow decided that the job really wasn't that important to him and quit on the spot.

Northwest view of the warden's house and old state prison store. *Courtesy Library of Congress, Prints and Photographs Division, HABS LA, 17-BATRO, 15-17 (ct).*

Several other workers, Mark included, often heard the sounds of walking on the second floor above them, but when they investigated, no one was ever found. Although on two separate occasions, fresh boot tracks were clearly seen in the dust on the floor where no one had been in some time. Talking was heard coming from the second floor as well, and several times the name Henry was clearly heard by everyone, just as it had been by the worker who quit.

Whether the spirits were there the entire time or the process of restoring the building simply stirred them up is impossible to say, but if I had to venture a guess, I would say that it was the renovations that brought on the occurrences. It's been noted for a long time in the paranormal community that spirits seem to become more active when renovations are happening. Whether it's simply that new eyes are there to see them or that they are upset with the changes being made, no one really knows for sure the reasoning behind it.

The Yard

Situated just a slight distance to the rear of the old prison store would have been the prison yard. Buildings now sit upon the site where prisoners once walked, talked and, upon occasion, killed each other. The prison, like most of the prisons of that era and even a few today, were violent places housing violent and sometimes completely sadistic and ruthless men who were incarcerated for a number of offenses from robbery and assault to murder. Simply because they were locked up away from society in no way meant that they were suddenly peaceful, rehabilitated men, and the level of violence that was experienced in the prisons only served to reinforce that fact. I spent a little time researching just how many men had been killed inside the prison facility in Baton Rouge from the time it was built until it was shut down in 1917, but while I am sure that there must be a record somewhere detailing the number of men killed, I was unable to find even a rough estimate of just how many prisoners had met their ends while incarcerated there. However, I was able to find a story here and there about a particular incident or two, one of which I think might be the origin of the ghost that haunts the area where the prison yard would have been.

As the story goes, in about 1878, a young man named Herbert was sent to the state prison for the crime of theft. He was accused of stealing a saddle and with the intent to steal a horse on which to use the saddle, as he had no horse of his own. Herbert was thought to be slightly mentally challenged since he didn't do much of anything other than mutter some unintelligible syllables during his trial. Although sentenced to two years, it was widely thought that due to his slight build and rather meek manner, he wouldn't last a month inside the prison walls. They couldn't have been more right, but not for the reason that he was meek. It seemed that he became a target for one individual in particular, Henre Thibodaux, who was locked up for beating a man to death with a singletree (a singletree was used to hitch a single horse to a wagon or plow). Henre was widely known as a cruel man and was given a pretty wide berth in the prison by both prisoners and guards alike. While it isn't known for sure, I suspect that he brutalized Herbert quite badly and repeatedly, for one day, Herbert just snapped. They were on the yard, and Henre started in berating Herbert and getting physical with him, tripping him and knocking him to the ground. Laughing, he turned his back and started to walk away. Herbert then leaped to his feet, and with a small piece of iron spring he had found somewhere, jumped on Henre's back and started stabbing him repeatedly in the side of the neck, effectively severing the artery and causing Henre to bleed to death there on the ground. A guard rushed up and struck Herbert in the head, and whether it was intentional or simply from adrenaline, the blow was solid and resulted in the death of Herbert, who lay on the ground next to the man he had just stabbed to death.

I'm sure not much was thought of the incident after a day or two, but slowly, people started talking about seeing Herbert's ghost. On more than one occasion, guards on duty in the evening hours reported seeing the ghost suddenly appear in the yard area only to disappear after walking a few steps. These sightings went on for a few years, many occurring at different times throughout the night. Then, one evening, a guard happened to be walking across the yard area and came face to face with Herbert.

Obviously startled by the sudden appearance of the man, as all of the prisoners were accounted for and locked up for the night, the guard reacted quickly and took a swipe at the prisoner with the wooden rod he was carrying. To his horror, the rod sliced right through the prisoner with no effect at all, save causing the prisoner to suddenly come to a halt in front of the guard. The ghost looked at the guard for a moment and then simply walked on through the man and disappeared a few steps away from him. Completely unnerved, the guard was reported to have quit on the spot.

The ghost of Herbert was spotted off and on even after the prison was closed and the main buildings and walls torn down. He would be seen walking a short distance and then fading away. Then, in about 1962, a young lady named Lila Courey was walking to her car one evening after work and was confronted by what could possibly have been the ghost of Herbert. She was walking down the sidewalk, digging in her purse for her car keys, when she became aware of someone in front of her. She drew up short, thinking she was about to bump into some one, and quickly looked up to say excuse me. What she saw caused her to gasp in surprise. Before her stood a dirty, unkempt young man with a vacant stare, his hands bloody and held up to his chest. As she gained her composure a bit, Lila let out a loud scream that, in her words, "would have rattled the windows for three city blocks." As she started to back away from him, the man suddenly reached out his hands toward her and then, without uttering a sound, faded from sight. That was all it took for Lila, who turned and ran full tilt, still screaming, back to her place of work. It took her several minutes to explain to her remaining co-workers what had just happened. A call was placed to the authorities, but after an extensive search, no one matching the description was found. The authorities determined that she must have run into a vagrant on the street and simply overreacted.

Lila, on the other hand, is convinced that what she encountered that evening was a ghost, and most likely one from the former prison. Although she said he never said a word and didn't try to harm her in any way, it was nonetheless one of the scariest events in her life to date, and one that she hopes to never experience again.

As the years have passed, fewer and fewer stories of encounters in the area have been reported, whether due to the extensive changes in the city landscape or simply from the spirits moving on, but every so often, someone will spot a ragged-looking person walking down the street who is there one minute and gone the next. Who knows, maybe it's a leftover prisoner from the old state prison?

CHAPTER 9

THE SPANISH MOON BAR

Sitting on Highland Road, the Spanish Moon Bar has a long and varied history. First built in the late 1800s, the building has been used as a feed store, a thrift store, a homeless shelter, several bars and twice as a morgue—once to hold bodies after a deadly flu epidemic hit the area in 1918 and again during the deadly floods of 1927. It is from its usage as a temporary morgue that the source of the hauntings are thought to have stemmed, although one spirit who has been seen in the building had more of a 1950s look about him, according to those who saw him.

Regardless of when the hauntings originated, numerous people over the years have witnessed more than just a few strange happenings in the Spanish Moon building.

CYPRESS HOLLOW TAVERN

Back in the 1970s and early 1980s, the building that now houses the Spanish Moon Bar was home to a tavern called Cypress Hollow. A typical beer bar, it had a good local following and by all accounts was a good working-class hangout—nothing special, just a place to knock back a couple of cold ones and relax in the evenings.

Margie had worked there for only a few weeks when she had her first—and only—experience with a handsome young ghost. When she had started

The Spanish Moon Bar building. *Photo by Hope Steed Kennedy.*

the job, she was told that sometimes things would happen that no one could explain, such as the beer taps suddenly turning on then off again, glasses sliding down the bar or across a tabletop only to fall to the floor (oddly enough, everyone who ever saw the glasses fall to the floor reported the same thing: they would land with a soft thud but never break) and the feeling of being bumped into.

Not one to get too shaken up over what she called "silly spook stories," Margie simply chuckled and brushed it off, enjoying her new job and making friends with the regulars and staff alike. One night, she was working the closing shift and was helping to clean up after the bar had closed when she started to get the feeling that she was being watched. Of course, there was no one in the building other than the bartender and herself, so she just shrugged it off as being tired and went back to getting the tavern in shape to open the next afternoon. As she was stacking glasses on the bar top, both she and the bartender watched as one of the beer taps slowly turned on. The bartender calmly reached over and pushed the tap back, smiled at Margie and said, "Happens all the time. Haven't figured out why just yet, as the taps not loose or anything, but it happens at least two to three times a night.

Maybe our ghost is thirsty or something." Margie said he chuckled a little as he walked away shaking his head. She wasn't sure if he was telling the truth or just trying to scare her, but either way, the work wasn't going to get done just standing there staring at the beer tap, so she went back to gathering and stacking glasses.

But Margie just couldn't shake the feeling of being watched. After about another fifteen to twenty minutes of work, Margie decided to take a quick bathroom break before wiping down the last of the tables. Standing in front of the mirror in the ladies' room, she looked up from washing her hands to see the reflection of a young man looking back at her in the mirror. Thinking someone had slipped in the bar and was now standing behind her, the startled Margie quickly spun around, but no one was there. She gingerly looked into the stall, half expecting someone to jump out at her, but no one was lurking there. Perplexed, she turned back around to see the reflection of the young man still standing there looking back at her from the mirror. She quickly checked behind her again, and although she saw no one, she could clearly see the reflection of the young man looking at her.

Just as she was about to let out a scream, the young man held up his hand, palm out, as if to say "stop" and then smiled a huge smile at her. Apparently, the effect was a calming one, as Margie said the scream died in her throat before she could even utter a sound. Now more curious than anything, she timidly reached her hand out toward the mirror where his hand was, not really sure what to expect. As she put her palm against the mirror, it appeared as if the young man did the same, smiling at her the whole time. As their hands seemed to meet on both sides of the mirror, she felt a slight electrical pulse, sort of like the tingle that you get when you put your tongue on both terminals of nine-volt battery. She told me that when she felt the tingle, she was immediately filled with a rush of emotions, as if she were experiencing everything he experienced. Happiness was the most profound feeling of them all, strangely enough, as if the young man was happy with where he was. Suddenly, with another wide smile, the reflection of the young man was gone, and Margie was left standing there feeling more than just a little bewildered at what had just happened.

In a daze, she wandered back out to the bar area, and the expression on her face caused the bartender to rush over to her out of concern that something was wrong. When she related the tale to him, he commented that he had caught a glimpse of the young man himself, peeking around the corner from the storeroom at him one afternoon. Thinking a customer had slipped back into the storeroom, he walked around the corner and into the storage area but found no one there.

Margie described the young man as being very good looking, with dark, wavy hair that reminded her of a young Elvis. He was wearing a white t-shirt with the sleeves rolled up and what looked to be jeans; he looked like he had just stepped off the screen from a 1950s movie. While startled at first, she said that she really wasn't scared after he had smiled at her. She thought he just looked like a happy nice young man.

Margie continued to work at the bar for a few more months before moving on to a better job and stated that although she felt as though she was being watched upon occasion, she never saw the young man again. She has often thought about going back to see if she might encounter him again but never has bothered to go, although she does wonder if he is still there and why exactly he seemed so happy to be in the tavern.

Over the years, quite a few people have experienced unexplainable encounters, including seeing a young man who is there one minute and gone the next; glasses moving, chairs moving on their own as if pulled away from the table so someone could set down; the feeling of being watched, touched and brushed up against; and the sound of someone whistling "It Wasn't God Who Made Honky Tonk Angels," which was originally recorded by Kitty Wells. Whoever the ghost might be, I like his taste in music.

CHAPTER 10

THE HILTON HOTEL
[HEIDELBERG HOTEL]

A short time after the huge floods of 1927, construction on the Heidelberg Hotel (now the Hilton Hotel), located at 201 Lafayette Street, was started. Inspections were done on the construction site each morning to check for groundwater seepage due to the flooding, but none was ever discovered and the building of the hotel went along quite smoothly.

The hotel began its life in the head of architect Edward Nield, and for the most part during the early stages of construction, that's where it stayed, with no more formal a set of plans than those drawn on a napkin. Nonetheless, it would be finished in grand style and would see many famous people grace its hallways. Presidents John F. Kennedy, Hubert Humphrey and Jimmy Carter would all stay at the hotel, as would numerous entertainers such as Will Rogers and Elvis Presley and many notable Louisiana politicians, including Governor Huey P. Long, who co-authored a song with Castro Carazo on the tenth floor.

The Heidelberg even saw a brief stint of service as the unofficial state capitol during a power struggle between Governor Huey P. Long and Lieutenant Governor Paul Cyr in 1931. Cyr declared it the state capitol when Long, who had won a United States Senate seat, refused to hand over control of the state to him. In 1935, Long would be assassinated in the hallway of the state capitol building by Dr. Carl Austin Weiss, although some people speculate that Long's own bodyguards actually shot him when they responded to the attack. Weiss would be killed himself moments later, the recipient of an estimated thirty or more bullet wounds.

The old Heidelberg Hotel, now known as the Hilton Hotel. *Photo by Hope Steed Kennedy.*

The Heidelberg suffered much neglect during the 1970s and was placed on the National Register of Historic Places in 1982 to save it from being torn down. The property has since been renovated and, along with the Capitol House, is now a part of the Hilton Hotel chain and is known as the Hilton Baton Rouge Capitol Center.

THE CIGAR-SMOKING GHOST

There seems to be several ghosts inhabiting the Heidelberg, and one has a distinct liking for cigars. Since the 1940s, many people have reported seeing the figure of a man strolling along the hallways smoking a cigar, seemingly in no hurry at all, just puffing away and walking at a leisurely pace. When approached or acknowledged, he will either fade from sight or first turn to look at the person who acknowledged him and then fade away. He seldom interacts with anyone, preferring the company of his cigars to that of other people.

Most of the sightings of the cigar smoker have been on the tenth floor of the hotel, prompting many to speculate that it is the ghost of former governor Huey P. Long, since he reportedly spent most of his time on that floor. However, Marvin, a former employee of the old Heidelberg Hotel who had a personal encounter with the cigar smoker, doesn't believe that it is the former governor. Just who it is, he has no idea, but he told me that he was face to face with the cigar-smoking ghost one night and that after looking at several photos of Governor Long, he is convinced that it isn't him.

Marvin was working as a nighttime security guard and was halfway through his shift when he had his encounter. He had just exited the stairway onto the tenth floor and started down the hallway when he noticed the smell of cigar smoke. Having worked at the hotel for a few years already, he was well familiar with the stories of the cigar-smoking ghost and had encountered the smell of cigar smoke on several other occasions. A believer in ghosts and hauntings, Marvin had never heard anything bad associated with the hauntings in the Heidelberg, so he wasn't overly concerned about it. Raised in what would be called a "spiritual household," Marvin's mother had instilled in him the notion that the dead were not necessarily to be feared but that they should be respected and that good manners were everything. So this time, like the others before, when he smelled the smoke, he simply said out loud, "I hope that you are enjoying your cigar and that you have a good night sir. I would be deeply appreciative if you would please try and not disturb the guests though."

You can imagine Marvin's surprise when he heard a man's voice behind him answer back, "Why thank you, and I will certainly do my best to remain quiet." Thinking that a guest had walked up behind him, he turned around to reply to the man only to find no one there at all. Smiling to himself, he turned back around to continue with his rounds, and there, a few feet in front of him, stood a man smoking a cigar. Marvin knew right away that it wasn't a real person in front of him; it was pretty apparent since there was just a swirling, and somewhat transparent black mass where his legs should have been. Marvin nodded his head at the man and said, "Good evening sir. Having a nice stay here at the Heidelberg?" The ghost smiled at Marvin and replied that he always enjoyed his stay at the hotel, and then he turned around and walked away, disappearing about halfway down the hallway.

Marvin said he just kind of stood there for a moment processing what had just happened before shrugging it off and continuing on his rounds. I asked him if he could describe the man that he had seen that night, and he told me that it was a middle-aged Caucasian man about five feet, nine inches tall with an average build and weight and sandy brown hair. He was wearing what looked like a grey wool suit with a white shirt and a bow tie and was sporting a thin mustache that stopped at the corners of his mouth. All in all, he stated that the man was a rather pleasant-looking fellow with a nice smile who seemed to be extremely polite and well mannered.

After hearing the detailed description of the ghost, I had to commend Marvin for being able to give such a detailed accounting, especially after so many years had passed. He told me that he would never forget what the man looked like—not because he was scared or anything, but because it was the first ghost he had ever seen face to face. He told me for years after the encounter he would look at every old photograph he happened upon to see if he might recognize the man in any of them but that he was never able to find out who he was. He never saw the cigar-smoking ghost again after that, although he would smell cigar smoke from time to time while making his rounds. He said that when he would smell the cigar smoke, he would have to smile a little to himself and say good evening to the man. After all, good manners are everything.

THE WHITE LADY

Another apparition that has been seen on occasion is that of the "White Lady," so named due to her snow-white gown and hair. She seems to like the dining and main salon areas in the early hours of the evening, although she was reported to have been encountered in a room on the third floor late one evening.

As the story goes, a husband and wife were staying at the hotel during a visit to Baton Rouge and had just returned from a night out on the town. Getting ready for bed, they walked out of the bathroom into the bedroom area to find a woman with white hair and dressed in a snow-white gown standing by the bed. From her appearance, she seemed to be distressed over something. Understandably startled, they immediately asked her who she was and what she was doing in their room. Looking confused, she ignored their questions and replied with one of her own, asking, "Who are you people and why are you in my room? You need to leave now—get out!"

Thinking that perhaps she was experiencing some type of mental breakdown, they tried to talk calmly to her while the husband edged closer to the phone, thinking that he would call the front desk and get someone up there to remove the woman and try to get her some help. As he reached for the phone, the woman flew into a fit of rage, screaming at them to get out of her room. And then, to the amazement of the couple, the woman rushed at them, passing completely through the bed. As she neared the man, he instinctively threw his hands up to stop her, but she passed completely through him and on through the wall behind him, screaming the entire time.

Needless to say, it took just a few seconds for the couple to get their wits back about them, and they nearly ripped the door off the hinges getting out of the room. They never broke stride, bypassing the elevators and taking the stairs to the bottom floor. Out of breath and as white as the ghost they had just seen, they slid to a stop in front of the check-in desk and proceeded to spill the story to a rather confused and concerned desk clerk. The desk clerk immediately dispatched security to the room, but no sign of anyone could be found, and the door handle and lock were working perfectly.

When offered another room, the couple quickly declined, and with security standing guard for them while they gathered their things and got dressed, they went back to the check-in desk, cleared their account and promptly left.

No one knows exactly who the woman is or why she haunts the hotel. Usually when she is seen, she simply fades away without any contact of any kind. Why she chose to interact with the couple and what her attachment, or perceived attachment, to the room was that night is anyone's guess.

CHAPTER 11
MAGNOLIA MOUND PLANTATION

L ocated at 2161 Nicholson Drive just a short distance from downtown Baton Rouge sits an incredible historic example of what life was like in the early years of the city. Once part of a nine-hundred-acre plantation that bordered the Mississippi River, it is now reduced to sixteen well-maintained acres managed by the Baton Rouge Recreation and Park Commission. Today, workshops, weddings, events and period historical functions are all held at Magnolia Mound, helping to provide a portion of the income required to maintain and operate the property. The property is open to the public Monday through Saturday, 10:00 a.m. to 4:00 p.m. and on Sundays from 1:00 p.m. to 4:00 p.m. More information about this wonderful piece of history can be found at www.brec.org and www.friendsofmagnoliamound.org.

HISTORY OF MAGNOLIA MOUND

The Magnolia Mound property was originally purchased by James Hillen, who arrived and settled in the Baton Rouge area around 1786. He would later sell the property to John Joyce, an Irish immigrant from County Cork, Ireland, just a few days before Christmas 1791. Joyce would build the house, a simple four-room cottage that was occupied by an overseer who managed the plantation, as John and his wife, Constance, actually lived in Mobile. John would later die from drowning in an attempt to cross a river near

Front view of the Magnolia Mound Plantation home. *Courtesy Library of Congress, Prints and Photographs Division, HABS LA, 17-BATRO, 14-1.*

Mobile while on a trip, leaving Constance a very wealthy widow with two children to raise.

Whether she met him on a trip to review her holdings at Magnolia Mound or in Mobile, Constance eventually made the acquaintance of Armand Duplantier, a wealthy landowner who owned a plantation across the river from Magnolia Mound and who was a prominent figure around Baton Rouge. Originally from France, he had served under the Marquis de Lafayette during the Revolutionary War and was known for having served with distinction. He was a widower with four children, and eventually the couple would be married and move their combined families to Magnolia Mound. The home was expanded and improved several times to better accommodate their family and the five more children they would have together.

They would furnish and decorate their home with imported wallpapers and silks, moldings, carved mantelpieces and paneling and would often make trips downriver to New Orleans, where they would purchase both imported and locally made furniture. With New Orleans being a major seaport at that

Parlor of the Magnolia Mound Plantation home. *Courtesy Library of Congress, Prints and Photographs Division, HABS LA, 17-BATRO, 14-10.*

time, quality items imported from all over the world could be found in the shops, available to the wealthy both in New Orleans and the surrounding communities and plantations. Magnolia Mound Plantation was outfitted expensively as befitted a wealthy planting family of that time.

But in addition to being a richly furnished and comfortable home, it was also a working plantation, with approximately fifty slaves farming cotton, sugar cane and subsistence crops on the remainder of the nine hundred acres. It is said that at one time, the plantation had sixteen cabins in which to house the slaves, although today, only one double slave cabin, or quarter house, remains on the property. It is not original to the plantation, though, having been a part of what was known as the Cherie Quarters on the old Riverlake Plantation and moved to its present location.

The plantation was pretty prosperous in the beginning, but sometime around 1814, things took a bit of a downturn for the family, who had to sell off various properties and holdings until they were left with just the Magnolia Mound property. In 1827, Armand would pass away, leaving Constance a widow once again. The plantation would stay in the Duplantier family for a while before also being sold off and passing through several families. By the late nineteenth century, the property was owned by a Mr. Louis Barillier, who eventually sold the land and all the improvements to a Mr. Robert A. Hart. Eventually, through family inheritance, Magnolia Mound made its way into the hands of Mrs. Blanche Duncan. She would commission the architectural firm of Goodman and Miller to make quite a few alterations and additions to the home around 1951, but by the 1960s, the house sat empty and was again in need of vast repairs. Thanks to the efforts of preservationists, the property was saved from demolition and was eventually purchased and restored by the Baton Rouge Recreation and Park Commission, opening to the public in 1975. The artifacts and furnishings displayed in the buildings of Magnolia Mound are owned by the Friends of Magnolia Mound Plantation and are representative of the period from 1802 to 1830, when the Duplantier family would have owned the property.

Today, the property boasts the main house, which is now home to a museum; a reconstructed open-hearth kitchen; an overseer's house which, while being original to the property itself was actually moved to its present location in 1977; a quarter house/double slave cabin; a carriage house; and a pigeonnier, which housed squabs and various other game birds that were staples of the plantation diet. A kitchen garden similar to what might have existed during the 1800s was designed and planted near the reconstructed open-hearth kitchen and is now used to produce food used in both the cooking demonstrations and educational tours about life on the plantation.

Should you ever get the opportunity to visit this remarkable piece of Louisiana history, you certainly will not be disappointed, as it provides an intimate glimpse into what life must have been like during the heyday of the great river plantations.

THE OVERSEER'S HOUSE

One of the few remaining buildings part of the original plantation, the overseer's house was moved from its location on Vermont Street to its current spot in 1977. Up until that time, the house had been sitting vacant from the time its last occupant, Mrs. Susie Martin White, passed away in the early '70s. Mrs. White was born in 1894 and was a descendant of slaves herself. A nice mention of her by her granddaughter can be read at the Friends of Magnolia Mounds Plantation website.

After the house was moved, it was restored and furnished as if still occupied by the overseer and his family. In addition to period furnishings, it is unique in that it also houses an early nineteenth-century sick room, a very interesting addition to the historical site.

One of the stories told to me about the overseer's house is that of someone softly singing. Several people have commented about hearing the sounds of a woman singing and humming old gospel tunes, very softly and quietly as one would almost do absentmindedly while going about some mundane task, coming from the house. Whenever someone would go inside to investigate, the singing would stop and all would be quiet again. Once the house was empty again, the sounds would continue, softly wafting across the open yard.

The sounds of someone walking about in the house have been heard quite a few times as well. A visitor to the plantation from Alexandria, Louisiana, told me that while standing just inside the front door, he distinctly heard the sounds of heavy footsteps walk right in front of him and his wife, as if someone with boots or hard-soled shoes had crossed the room. A curious sort of fellow, he went on into the room (although his wife declined to accompany him into the house) and followed in the general direction that the footsteps seemed to go. As he passed into another room, he felt as though he had passed through a huge amount of spider webs, although none could be seen, and the temperature of the room dropped significantly, enough to raise goose bumps on his arms. He said it lasted for just a moment and then was gone, the temperature returning to normal. He walked around the rest of the house but didn't experience anything else unusual. He thinks that what he experienced was possibly a brief encounter with a previous occupant of the home still going about his routine.

Some of the other things experienced at the overseer's house are the sounds of footsteps on the front porch area, not heavy ones like what the gentleman and his wife from Alexandria experienced, but soft and light, as if from someone small or barefoot. On occasion, the faint sounds of someone

Drawn plans of the pigeonnier at Magnolia Mound Plantation. *Courtesy Library of Congress, Prints and Photographs Division, HABS LA, 17-BATRO, 14a.*

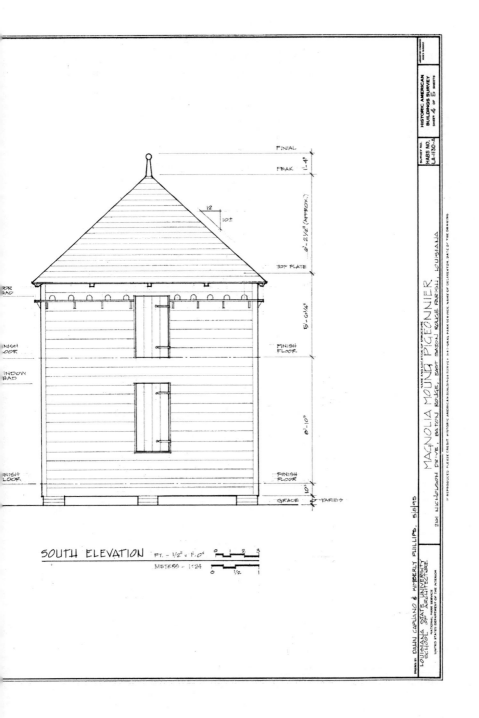

SOUTH ELEVATION

talking can also be heard coming from both the front and rear of the house. It's been described as soft, almost like a mumble, and those who have heard it can never quite make out what is being said. The same soft mumbling has been heard in the vicinity of the pigeonnier, which was not a part of the original plantation, being donated by the Barthel family from their property near Sunshine, Louisiana.

All in all, there seems to be a slight bit of activity going on in the overseer's house at Magnolia Mound Plantation—not enough to really scare someone, but just enough to let you know that perhaps some of the former occupants might still be hanging around.

THE QUARTER HOUSE

The quarter house, an 1830's slave house that was originally part of the Cherie Quarters on the Riverlake Plantation, seems to have some mild paranormal occurrences happening in and around it as well. As with the overseer's house, the sounds of soft singing and humming have been heard, although it is so faint that the tune can't quite be determined. In the early evening, the sounds of what seem to be people moving about in the furnished side of the house have been heard, although no one is ever found whenever it has been investigated. Late at night, people have glimpsed what appear to be shadow people moving about in the yard only to fade away after traveling a few steps. Described as being dressed in mismatched clothing and barefoot, the figure of an African American man has been seen entering the quarter house on several occasions. It was thought that he was a reenactor by those visitors who saw him, but upon investigation, no one could be found in the house. Who he is or was is anyone's guess, I suppose. Perhaps he is attached to the house, a former occupant from when it was located on Riverlake Plantation.

One other thing that I would like to mention that has been seen at both the quarter house and toward the rear of the property is what is generally referred to as a "spook light." On several occasions, a small ball of light has been seen flitting about the slave house at night, sometimes moving quickly and other times just poking along. At first glance, it appears to be someone walking with a flashlight, but those who have seen it have commented on its erratic movements and how the light will pulse before flaring up and nearly fading away. The light is usually seen in the early morning hours, and after moving about the slave quarters, it will meander off toward the back of the property. Lights such as these have been seen all over the world in a number of places ranging from graveyards to historical buildings to, in the case of the Joplin Spook Light near Joplin, Missouri, the middle of nowhere. There are numerous guesses as to what the cause of the lights might be, including everything from swamp gas, spirits and large masses of lightning bugs to off-the-wall speculations such as fairies or aliens. No one knows for sure what might be causing the mysterious lights; they seem to fade quickly from sight before anyone can get close enough to try and determine what they might be. My opinion is that they are simply some form of spirit manifestation, and I always thought that it would be interesting to place an infrared camera, such as a game or trail camera that's triggered by motion, near a place where it's been seen multiple times to see if an image of the anomaly might be captured.

THE MAIN HOUSE

Originally built in the 1790s, the main house at Magnolia Mound has been beautifully restored and is home to a large collection of period items owned by the Friends of Magnolia Mound Plantation. The home is now a museum, and the items are on permanent display, giving an accurate and historical glimpse into what life must have been like for a wealthy plantation owner and his family in the early 1800s. Much care has been taken throughout the home—and the entire complex, for that matter—to provide visitors with an educational view of the day-to-day existence during that period.

One of the thoughts associated with paranormal research is that spirits can and will attach themselves to items to which they had an emotional attachment in life. Many times we have been called by a frantic homeowner who was suddenly experiencing everything from seeing ghosts to doors opening and closing by themselves to learn that they had just brought a new treasure home from the flea market or estate sale. Usually, when the item was removed from the home, the experiences stopped. Well-known paranormal investigator and researcher John Zaffis has built up a huge paranormal museum from haunted items that he has removed from people's homes. With that being said, when you have historical buildings that are full of authentic period items (such as those at Magnolia Mound), it's hard to determine if the hauntings and sightings are from those people who were once a part of the plantation or those who might be there simply due to an attachment to an item on display. Without a series of well-conducted investigations we likely will never really know the identities of those spirits seen and heard at Magnolia Mound Plantation.

For example, one sighting, that of a man standing near the fireplace in the parlor, could be anyone from Duplantier or another former owner to someone simply attached to an item in the home. However, a few clues help to narrow it down a bit, as those who have seen the man describe him as wearing tan-colored riding pants, knee-high black boots, a white shirt and a short black waistcoat. He was said to be rather short by today's standards, maybe five and a half feet or so, with mutton-chop sideburns, which were quite popular back in the 1800s, and dark, wavy hair. Most times, he has been seen through the window standing by the fireplace and is immediately mistaken for a reenactor. But when visitors enter the room, no trace of him can be found, as he seems to have simply disappeared. On several occasions, he has been seen pacing back and forth as if in deep thought. He appears to be talking to himself or some other unseen person in the room. Once again,

West porch of the restored Magnolia Mound Plantation home. *Courtesy Library of Congress, Prints and Photographs Division, HABS LA, 17-BATRO, 14-19 (ct).*

those who have seen him have mistaken him for a reenactor who is simply pacing the floor while rehearsing his lines. As far as I have been able to find out, no one has ever had any direct contact with the man; he is simply gone when they enter the room.

Other experiences at the main house include doors opening and closing on their own, the sound of footsteps in the parlor area, small items that seem to move by themselves, phantom laughter and the sound of people talking. Several people have also told of seeing a small boy, his age estimated to be about five or six, playing in the yard at the rear of the main home. Apparently, he's there one minute and gone the next. Those who have seen him have commented on how he seems to be laughing and playing, yet they never hear a sound coming from him, which I find to be a little creepy.

From the accounts I have heard, none of the spirits that call the Magnolia Mound Plantation home are malevolent. Instead, they seem to be rather comfortable in their existence there, not really reaching out to or interacting with the living much at all. If the stories are to be believed, they seem to be rather content with how things are. I, for one, would certainly like to conduct a formal investigation of the three homes on the property to see what kind of audio or photographic evidence might be obtained. It would be interesting to see if we might be able to put a name to the man pacing the parlor floor.

CHAPTER 12

ST. JAMES EPISCOPAL CHURCH

There are really only two stories that I have heard in connection with this beautiful church, both being quite nice in my opinion and a testament to the bond that people of faith can establish with their church. While neither story is particularly scary or stems from a horrific act, I thought it was important to include them (one of which I experienced myself while slipping inside to check out the interior of the church) in this accounting.

In 1820, a charter was granted for an "Episcopal Congregation of Baton Rouge," with the standing length of the charter being ten years. However, the charter was never renewed, and in 1843, after a visit from Bishop Leonidas Polk, often referred to as the "Fighting Bishop of the Confederate Army," the church was officially reorganized. In 1845, construction was started on a wood-frame church, but by the 1880s, the congregation was outgrowing the little wooden church. In 1889, architect Colonel W.L. Stevens and a contractor by the name of W.H. Miller began construction of the Gothic Revival–style church that you see today. Finished in 1895, it is a beautiful church, with the exterior made of locally manufactured brick and the interior sporting a mix of cypress and pine. In my opinion, however, the most beautiful feature of all is the hammer-beam mahogany ceiling, the largest span in the nave being approximately thirty-five feet.

One famous connection that the church had was that of Zachary Taylor, who would go on to be the twelfth president of the United States. Taylor moved his wife, Margaret, to Baton Rouge before setting off to fight in

Interior of St. James Episcopal Church. *Courtesy Library of Congress, Prints and Photographs Division, HABS LA, 17-BATRO, 10-11.*

the Mexican-American War, where he distinguished himself by taking the supposedly impregnable city of Monterrey in three short days. Margaret attended services at St. James regularly, as did Zachary when he returned.

The church continued to grow with the addition of adjoining properties over the years to become a fairly large complex of buildings encompassing the entire block.

BRIGADIER GENERAL THOMAS WILLIAMS

Thomas Williams was promoted to the rank of brigadier general in September 1861 and was assigned as the commander of the Union forces in Baton Rouge on May 29, 1862. He was considered by those who knew him to be a decent and caring man albeit a rather strict disciplinarian when it came to matters of military nature. He regularly attended the St. James Episcopal Church during his three-month stay in Baton Rouge, and in fact, he had attended that same church the Sunday before he died in the Battle of Baton Rouge, which took place on August 5 of that year. He was grievously wounded in the chest during the defense of the city and was taken to the home of some members of the church, who cared for him until he passed. It's said that while he lay there dying, he expressed his gratitude to the church and its members for accepting him into their fold and for caring for him in his time of need. He then dictated a short note to his family and expressed his wish that they remember St. James Episcopal Church and the care that they had extended him. In October 1887, a granite baptismal font was donated to the church by the brigadier general's son. A large and ornately carved font made in the Eastlake style, it is located in the northern transept of the church.

My reason for telling the story of Brigadier General Williams and the donated font is that on several occasions, a man in a Union military uniform has been seen standing next to it. He is said to simply stand there touching the font while smiling, as if pleased with what he sees. After a brief moment or two, he turns to walk away and then simply fades from sight. Perhaps the brigadier general returns occasionally to check on the baptismal font that was donated in his memory, or maybe he just stops by to pay his respects to a church that took in an enemy soldier and cared for him until his passing. Either way, I think it's a rather nice testament to the church and the values it espouses.

THE LADY IN THE PEW

Although I had heard this story once before, I actually experienced this myself back in 1992 when I was passing through Baton Rouge and decided to stay and visit with my younger brother and his family. I have always had a passion for photography and was out walking about taking photos when I paused to take some images of the outside of the St. James Episcopal Church. As I snapped a

Front view of St. James Episcopal Church. *Courtesy Library of Congress, Prints and Photographs Division, HABS LA, 17-BATRO, 10-16 (ct).*

few images of the front of the church, I decided that I was going to see if the door was open so that I could get a look inside. I figured any church that impressive on the outside must be extremely beautiful on the inside. As luck would have it, the door was unlocked, so I eased inside to have a look, hoping that I wasn't going to be interrupting a service or wedding or something. As I walked into the church, I was awestruck by the ceiling beams, the stained-glass windows and how perfect everything looked. And by perfect I mean that the interior layout was perfect—everything was in line and in perfect proportion. As I was standing there, I noticed an elderly lady sitting in one of the rear pews, her head bowed as if in prayer or reflection, so I quietly moved to the side and discreetly snapped a few photos of the pews running in a perfect line toward the altar. Not wanting to bother her, I walked over to the far side of the church and walked down toward the altar area intending to take a few more photos of it and the beautiful Tiffany stained-glass windows behind it. As I was walking, I glanced back to where the lady was sitting to see her still there, head still bowed in prayer. I went ahead and took my photos and started back along the opposite wall. As I drew close to her, she raised her head and looked at me, and I immediately apologized for disturbing her. She smiled at me and said that I hadn't bothered her at all, to which I expressed my relief and then remarked to her on how beautiful the church was and asked if she was a member there. She smiled and said that she was a member of the congregation and agreed that it was a very beautiful church and probably the most peaceful place she had ever been.

As I stood at the end of the pew talking with her, I couldn't help but notice how peaceful she seemed, and for some reason, I was reminded of my grandmother for a moment and felt just a little sad. My grandmother had raised me from the time they brought me home from the hospital until the day she died, when I was ten years old. I guess it must have shown a bit on my face because the elderly lady smiled at me once again and simply said, "She misses you, too."

It took a moment for what she had just said to register with me, and before I could reply, she stood up and said, "Well, I have to go now. May God bless you and keep you safe." And with that she turned away, stepped out into the aisle and faded away right in front of my eyes. I was simply rooted to the spot for a moment. I had been investigating the paranormal for roughly ten years by that point and had seen some unexplainable things, but she seemed so real! I had thought the whole time that I had been visiting with someone's sweet old grandmother, not a ghost of congregations past.

As I gathered my thoughts and myself together, I simply didn't know what to make of it, so I quietly replied to her blessing with, "And may God bless you as well." I snapped a few more photos of the inside of the church and then quietly left the building, suddenly feeling very peaceful and happy myself—the first time in quite a while actually.

As I walked down the sidewalk, I suddenly remembered the story I had heard several years earlier from a young woman who had visited St. James Episcopal Church to take photos, just as I had. While there, she encountered what she described as "the sweetest little old lady I have ever met." Much the same as my encounter, she spoke with an elderly lady who was sitting in a back pew, traded pleasantries and then walked with her toward the door of the church. As they neared the door, the elderly woman stopped and turned to the young woman, placed her hand on her arm and said, "It's all going to be ok dear. God bless you." Then she turned away from the young woman and faded away right before her eyes. The young woman confided in me that she never felt the least bit scared by what had happened; if anything, it was just the opposite.

I have no idea who the elderly lady was, only that she claimed to be a member of the congregation and that she shared my opinion on just how remarkably beautiful the church was. The only thing I can say with certainty was that at that time in my life, I was struggling with some doubts about God and religion in general, stemming from my research into ghosts and hauntings and from some of the things that I had witnessed during investigations. I was beginning to doubt if there was anything good left in this world. I think that perhaps the elderly lady was simply there to let me know that in spite of all the bad things that I had witnessed and dealt with trying to help people understand their paranormal experiences, there were just as many, if not more, good entities and spirits out there trying to bring a bit of peace to those who were struggling.

I have not been back inside the church since that day, but I think about the elderly lady from time to time, especially when I have been dealing with a lot of stressful stuff, and just replaying that experience in my head makes me feel so much better every time. I hope to someday go back to St. James Church to have another look around and maybe sit for a while in quiet contemplation in one of the rear pews. Maybe I'll be fortunate enough to get to visit with her again.

CHAPTER 13

THE OLD
COTTAGE PLANTATION

Located just south of Baton Rouge along the River Road are the ruins of what was once a grand plantation house. Built around 1824 by Colonel Abner Duncan as a present for his daughter and her husband, Frederick Daniel Conrad, it was presented to them on their wedding day and was considered by many to be the finest plantation home in the area. Sitting on a slight rise of ground just a little east of the levee that separated it from the Mississippi River, this grand home sported twenty-two rooms on two floors, all of which opened onto wraparound porches. It was exactly the type of home that one imagines a grand plantation home would look like, complete with eight columns across both the front and back and four columns across each side.

As one would imagine, furnishings and accoutrements befitting a family of wealth were brought in from New Orleans and from Europe, and the home was decorated richly and in the high style of the times. By all accounts, the family was very successful in their business dealings. They had amassed a considerable fortune, and they were not shy about using it to improve their living conditions.

The Conrad family hosted many notables of the time, including the Marquis de Lafayette; Zachary Taylor and his wife, Margaret; Jefferson Davis; and Henry Clay. They were a prominent and well-liked family in the Baton Rouge community.

Sometime in the 1850s, a man by the name of Ezra Holt (I have also found him referred to as Esa Holt, so I am not too sure which is the correct first name) came to live at the Cottage Plantation. I have also found several conflicting accounts of his position at the Cottage Plantation. One states that he was employed by Mr. Conrad as a teacher for his children, while another has him listed as a gardener. I would imagine that given the time period and the affluence of the Conrad family, he was most likely hired as a teacher and probably performed some personal secretarial services for Mr. Conrad as well.

As the story goes, when the Civil War broke out and Union troops began flooding into the area, the Cottage Plantation was occupied by Union forces. Here again, I have found two differing stories of the occupation. One states that the family was literally held prisoner in the home, their possessions seized and carried away and both Mr. Conrad and Mr. Holt being brutalized and beaten quite regularly by the Union troops. Another account states that the occupying Union troops merely camped on the plantation grounds and that the officers were received by the Conrads and given accommodations at the home. I tend to go with the last account myself simply from the point that the Conrad family was well connected and could even trace their ancestry back to George and Martha Washington. They had hosted many notable and prominent people who would later go on to hold positions of importance on both sides of the Civil War, so it is unlikely that they would have been brutalized if for no other reason than the occupying officers fearing reprisal and damage to the military careers. And in addition to that, it simply wasn't the convention of the time—respect was shown to women, and men conducted themselves with honor, at least in the early part of the war. No, while some things such as food might have been appropriated, I find it highly unlikely that everything of value would have been carried off when the Union troops moved on.

Mr. Conrad, recognizing that the war was not going to be over quickly, moved his family to New Orleans for the duration of the war, and he eventually died there. The plantation was said to have been taken over by Union forces shortly after the Conrad family left and was used as a hospital to treat the wounded from nearby battles and those who contracted yellow fever, a very common illness of the time. It's been said and is most likely true that there are numerous Union soldiers buried on the plantation grounds, victims of wounds and the fever. After the war, the Union troops pulled out, leaving the plantation house sitting vacant, and it's probably the fact that it served as a yellow fever clinic that saved it from being vandalized and torn down; many people were afraid that remnants of the disease might be lying dormant within its walls.

According to the story, the threat of disease didn't stop Mr. Holt from returning and taking up residence at the old plantation house. But those who knew him said that he returned as a changed man. He seemed totally fixated on repairing and maintaining the house for the remaining Conrad family members and with keeping trespassers away from the property. He remained at the property until the day he died, becoming something of a recluse. The fact that he had stopped shaving and grew a long white beard only added to the strangeness of what the man had become, since most who remembered him recalled that he had been a kind, neat and fastidious man. Some of the local people who knew him surmised that his mind was starting to wander due to his age, and they started leaving gifts of food for him to ensure that he at least had enough to eat.

When he finally passed away, the Holt family made sure that he received a proper burial, and all were in attendance to pay their last respects to a man who had been their teacher, friend and caretaker throughout their lives. With his passing, the Cottage Plantation would once again sit empty, although the local consensus was that the ghost of Holt was still watching over the property. It was nearly impossible to find anyone in the area that would go near the old house in the daytime, let alone at night. People who passed by the old house frequently noted a man with a long white beard that looked remarkably like Holt standing on the upper balcony looking out toward the River Road. Those brave enough to enter the house encountered doors that would slam shut on their own, ice-cold breezes that seemed to pass right through them and a loud voice shouting, "Get out!" Apparitions and dark shadow figures were seen walking the grounds both during the day and at night, and the ghost of a Union soldier was said to stand next to the front entrance as if on guard duty. Yes, the local consensus of that time was that the old Cottage Plantation home was indeed haunted.

Sometime during the 1920s, the Cottage Plantation experienced a much-needed restoration, with members of the Conrad family hoping to restore the home to its former glory. By the 1950s, the home had been restored and was opened as a museum dedicated to the memory of the Old South, giving people a glimpse into life as it was before the Civil War. The home attracted a good number of visitors, and according to one account, it was used as the set for several movies, including *Band of Angels*, which starred Clark Gable.

Even with the home restored to its former glory, the stories of ghosts still persisted, with visitors encountering the figure of a stooped old man with a long white beard, Union soldiers and the sounds of music and singing coming from the house and grounds. Several people claimed to have photographs of the ghost of Mr. Holt looking out from the upper balcony, and while it is highly possible that they do, I have not been able to track any of them down and have yet to see one myself.

In February 1960, a fire broke out in the old house, and while firemen valiantly fought to save the old plantation home, it burned completely down to the ground. One story about the fire holds that several firemen who were on the scene reportedly saw an old man with a white beard looking out the upstairs window at them, but before he could be rescued, the roof collapsed. When the debris was sifted through after the fire, no body was found, and it was speculated that it was the ghost of Mr. Holt looking out at them, still watching over the home.

All that remains of the once-grand home are some brick columns in the middle of a field, reminiscent of the Windsor Ruins located between Port Hudson and Rodney, Mississippi. The property holding the ruins of the Cottage Plantation is blocked off from trespassers by an electric fence. Those brave enough to slip under the fence to get a closer look at the ruins have reported seeing an old man standing near the columns; however, when approached, he vanishes from sight. Others have reported being touched or grabbed on the arm; hearing whispered voices that sounded as if they were right next to their ear; being pushed from behind; hearing the sounds of laughter, singing and music as if a party were taking place; and experiencing an overall feeling of sadness and loss. Perhaps the spirits that remain on the property and within the ruins of the old Cottage Plantation simply want to mourn the loss of their way of life in peace, without the intrusion of the curious. While the paranormal investigator part of me would like nothing better than to set up shop there some night to see what evidence might be captured, another part of me feels that perhaps we should just let them alone to go on about their business as they choose.

CHAPTER 14
ST. JOSEPH
CATHOLIC CEMETERY

The Diocese of New Orleans was established in 1793 and encompassed the area from New Orleans north to include Baton Rouge. A Catholic parish had already been established in Baton Rouge a year earlier, the Church of Our Lady of Sorrows, which would later be renamed St. Joseph. Construction on the current church was started in 1853 and finished up about 1855, although it has been renovated and updated many times since.

St. Joseph's was declared a cathedral in 1961 when Pope John XXIII established the Diocese of Baton Rouge, making St. Joseph's the center of the new diocese—a complex that takes up the entire block.

THE CEMETERY

The historical marker in front of St. Joseph's cemetery reads:

> *In 1825, St. Joseph Church purchased this property for a graveyard. Remains of some of Baton Rouge's first settlers were moved here from the old Spanish Cemetery, or cemetery of the Church of Our Lady of Sorrows, which became St. Joseph's. Philip Hicky, Adreen Persac, and Theophile Allain are among prominent Louisianans buried here. The Catholic Diocese of Baton Rouge owns the cemetery.*

Historical marker at St. Joseph's Catholic Cemetery. *Photo by Hope Steed Kennedy.*

The old Spanish Cemetery, or the cemetery of the Church of Our Lady of Sorrows, was located near where the current complex of buildings that make up the Diocese of Baton Rouge are now located. With the growth of the city and buildings springing up all around them, it was thought to be in the best interest of the city and all involved if a new piece of land was purchased, consecrated and made use of as a cemetery to hold the remains of the faithful. The bodies in the old Spanish Cemetery were reinterred at St. Joseph's that same year, and the cemetery currently holds some of the oldest graves in the area, including those of many prominent members of early Baton Rouge society. As the historical marker points out, some famous Louisianans are entombed there, including Theophile Allain, who was born from the union of a slave mother and plantation-owner father. Allain was treated as free and accompanied his father nearly everywhere, including Europe, and received the finest education available. He went on to become a successful businessman and served in the Louisiana House of Representatives from 1872 to 1874 and from 1881 to 1890, with a term in the Senate from 1874 to 1880. He supported what was known as the

Tombs at St. Joseph's Catholic Cemetery. *Photo by Hope Steed Kennedy.*

Unification Movement, which promoted an alliance of both black and white moderates to bring about changes in favor of the working class. He passed away in 1917 and was buried at St. Joseph's in what was described as a "funeral fit for a King" and attended by hundreds of mourners.

St. Joseph's Cemetery is a quiet and peaceful place of rest visited by many people who wander around the gravesites taking in the history to be found there. Unfortunately, some people get a little bit closer to history than they counted on.

THE GRAVEDIGGER

Burials in some parts of Louisiana, including New Orleans and some areas of Baton Rouge, are most usually done above ground because 1) the area is prone to flooding and 2) the early Spanish tradition of using vaults to entomb their dead has survived throughout the years. But not everybody was buried above ground when they passed away; some were buried directly in the ground as deep as they could go, depending on the water table, while others were buried in a sort of mix of the two. Today, with lead-lined, completely sealed vaults and securely sealed caskets, underground burial is not so much an issue. But back in the day, it wasn't so simple, and care had to be taken to ensure the proper burial of the deceased. The grave would be dug, and the walls and floor of the vault would be laid out using bricks and mortar, the walls usually rising a foot or so above ground level. When the owner of the gravesite would pass away, his casket would be lowered into the vault, sitting on several pillions made of brick to ensure that if a little ground water should seep in, the casket would remain high and dry. The slab, or top cap, would then be set in place.

Most people didn't have the skill to build below-ground vaults, so the services of a gravedigger would be employed. He would dig the grave, lay out the floor and the walls and temporarily put the top cap in place—most likely so that no one would accidentally fall into the vault. Then, on the day of the burial, he would return to remove the top cap and then permanently put it back in place after the casket had been placed inside.

I recall one story told to me a few years back when we were on vacation and were staying for a few days near Natchez, Mississippi. After dinner, I was sitting out on the front porch of the nice little bed and breakfast we were staying in, just relaxing a bit before I ventured off to check out some of the more haunted spots around Natchez. An older man and his wife were staying at the bed and breakfast with us, and they came out on the porch and politely asked if they could join us. We of course said yes, and we started engaging in small talk as strangers often do. The conversation steered itself around to ghosts and hauntings (the bed and breakfast we were staying at was supposedly haunted, but I didn't witness anything out of the ordinary), and I mentioned that I was a paranormal investigator and researcher and that I was going to go out and take a walk to check out some of the alleged paranormal hotspots of the town. The gentleman laughed a bit and told me that if it was ghosts I wanted to find, then I should check out the St. Joseph's Cemetery in Baton Rouge. He said that he and his wife had seen what could only be described as a nineteenth-century gravedigger, complete with lantern and an old wood-handled shovel. Well naturally he had captured my interest with the word "cemetery," so I asked him if he wouldn't mind sharing their story with me, as I had family in Baton Rouge and was very familiar with the city.

It would seem that the gentleman and his wife were now slightly amused at what they had seen, although both readily admitted to being quite frightened when they saw the gravedigger. They admitted that they were a couple who appreciated history and that one of the hobbies they shared was that of gravestone rubbing, where you take a plain white piece of paper and a piece of charcoal and rub over the inscription or design of the stone to make a copy of it. You then spray the paper with either hairspray or a similar product from an art supply store to keep

View of the cemetery grounds, St. Joseph's Catholic Cemetery. *Photo by Hope Steed Kennedy.*

the charcoal image from smudging. This process is used quite frequently by genealogists to help preserve death records from headstones that are starting to deteriorate. They told me that they had a collection of over 3,500 different gravestone rubbings, some from as far away as Germany and Ireland.

They said they had been walking about the St. Joseph Cemetery early one evening looking for unique gravestone designs and/or inscriptions when the wife remarked to her husband that she felt like she was being watched and had been for some time. He replied that he had been feeling the same way but that after looking around and not seeing anyone, he had simply brushed it off. They both continued on looking for something unique to copy for their collection, pausing here and there to read the dates and short inscriptions, but they had yet to find anything that was overly interesting. As they stopped for a brief moment under a tree next to a burial vault, they suddenly heard a man's voice on the other side of the tree ask them what they were doing.

They were startled but thought that perhaps they had just failed to notice the man when they walked up. The husband moved around the tree to see who it was that was on the other side, but there was no one there. Walking completely around the tree, the couple exchanged looks that clearly asked, "You heard that too, right?" They continued to look around them to see if they might see someone, thinking that maybe someone was simply playing

111

a joke on them, but after a few minutes of not seeing anyone, they decided to move on for a bit more exploring of the cemetery. They stopped at one aboveground vault that had a very interesting design that included a fleur-de-lis symbol worked into it, and while they were preparing to make their copy, they once again heard a man's voice ask them what they were doing. They spun around, but as before, there was no one standing there, although both had heard the voice just as clearly as if the person had been standing right next to them. A little nervous now, they decided to go ahead and get the copy of the design and then leave, not entirely sure exactly what was happening. As they taped the paper down with painter's tape and prepared to do the rubbing, they heard the voice say, "I asked you twice now just what you think you are doing snooping around my cemetery. I won't ask you again!"

As before, they spun around, only this time there stood an older-looking fellow holding onto a shovel and what looked to be an old-time lantern—one of those lanterns that use a candle and reflector to produce light. The gentleman chuckled a little bit now as he told me the story, referring to the figure before him as "an escaped character from an old Scooby Doo cartoon," complete with stringy hair, ill-fitting clothing and large, extremely dirty hands. And while he might have chuckled a bit then, he assured me that no one even cracked so much as a smile when it was happening. He said the man had a very menacing look about him, as if he might be slightly unhinged.

"We were just making a rubbing of the design on this gravestone is all," the woman stammered, backing up as far as she could go without climbing up and over the vault. "We meant no harm or disrespect, I can assure you."

"Well, the priest isn't going to like you snooping around out here," the old man replied. "I suggest you get out of my cemetery right now."

By this time, the husband was sufficiently recovered from being startled by the old man and was starting to get just a bit peeved about the whole thing. He informed the old man that they were not doing anything wrong, that they had done rubbings in cemeteries all over the world and that they were not leaving until they were done. "Just who the heck do you think you are anyway?" the husband asked him.

The older man raised his shovel up and took a threatening step toward them and said, "I am the gravedigger at this here cemetery, and I am telling you to get out. The priest isn't going to like you being here!" By the end of the sentence, the older man was practically screaming at the couple, shaking the old shovel up and down like a javelin thrower getting ready for competition.

"Let's just go honey, let's just go," the man's wife begged him, obviously scared by what was happening. But by that time, the man was fighting mad, and he told me at that point he was damned if he was going to let some half-baked old reprobate who looked like he had just stepped out of a cartoon order him off the property like a common trespasser.

"We're not going anywhere mister, so I suggest you just back the hell off and leave us alone," the man told the gravedigger. "We'll leave when we are good and ready to go and not one damn minute sooner!"

By this time, the woman was completely sure that they were going to be killed and buried in the cemetery by this crazy old man and was literally begging her husband to leave. He had his Irish up though, and he had no intention of tucking tale and running for the car—not at that point anyway.

The old man started pacing back and forth in front of them muttering to himself and shaking the shovel up and down, completely agitated by that time. Suddenly, he stopped and glared at the couple standing with their backs to the burial vault with what the woman described as pure evil, as if the very devil himself were about to burst from out of him.

"So you're not going to leave, huh? Think you can just do whatever you want whenever you want to, do you? Think you're better than me, don't you? Well, maybe it's time someone taught you some damn manners!" And with that, he suddenly launched himself at the couple, swinging the shovel like a club, intent on killing the both of them it seemed. The man instinctively threw his hands up to try and stop the shovel, stepping in front of his wife to protect her. What happened next completely freaked them both out so bad that after a moment, they both scrambled over the top of the burial vault and ran as fast as they possibly could to the relative safety of their car.

As the man stepped in front of his wife and braced his arms to try and catch the blow of the shovel, the shovel passed completely through him as if it was nothing but air, leaving only a bitter cold feeling in its passing. Dumbfounded, they both stood there for a moment as the gravedigger pulled back his shovel and let out a loud evil cackle of a laugh that broke the spell they were under and sent them running like the very hounds of hell were on their trail.

They reached their car in a panic and tore away as fast as they could, the man remarking to me that it was simply amazing that they didn't hit something or kill someone with their erratic driving. They drove back to the hotel they were staying at, and not ones to take a drink (according to them anyway), they went straight to the hotel bar and ordered a couple of shots to take the edge off. They told me that they didn't sleep a wink at all that night, afraid that every noise in the room was going to turn out to be the gravedigger getting ready to take another swing at them with his phantom shovel. They left early the next morning, and at the time that I had visited with them on the porch of the bed and breakfast in Natchez, they hadn't been back to Baton Rouge since. The gentleman's wife said that she was reasonably sure they never would either.

I found the story to be very interesting simply because in all of my years of researching and investigating the paranormal, I have never heard of a homicidal grave-digging ghost who hangs out in cemeteries. Of course, that doesn't mean that I don't believe their story; it just means that it's the first one of its kind that I have come across. Having been to St. Joseph's Catholic Cemetery on several occasions, the first time being many years ago to take some photographs for a project that I started and never got around to finishing, I always found it to be a peaceful and quiet place of rest, and nothing about it ever felt threatening to me at all. Of course, I wasn't touching the headstones and burial vaults either.

CHAPTER 15
GHOSTS OF LSU

No book of ghost stories about Baton Rouge would be complete without giving a short nod to the ghosts supposedly haunting the campus of Louisiana State University. The stories are most likely urban legends created during a party to try and scare the girls and nothing more. They run the same gamut as the stories associated with nearly every major university in the country—those of lost love and murder/suicide, accidental hanging during hazing, binge-drinking ghosts and a whole plethora of supposedly ghostly happenings.

I am only going to touch briefly on a few of them, as they really don't merit much attention, but they are as much a part of the campus as a math book or football and have been told and retold to each successive incoming class by those already familiar with the tales.

PLEASANT HALL

As the legend goes, Pleasant Hall used to be the girls' dormitory back in the 1970s and was the site of more than one campus hookup. Late at night, it wasn't uncommon for some of the boys to sneak in to spend a little "quality time" with their girlfriends on the weekends. One such couple is the subject of this tale and has been referred to over the years as "Mike and Sue" when the story is told.

It would seem that Sue, although extremely pretty, was a little high strung and had a bit of a quick temper, while Mike was the good-looking all-American boy. It was love at first sight for the two, and they went everywhere together and did everything as a couple. Everyone who knew them had no trouble believing that wedding bells would ring for them sometime in their near future—however, it turns out it would be more like a funeral dirge than wedding bells.

Mike started sneaking in to spend time with Sue in her room on the third floor of Pleasant Hall. It turns out that one thing led to another, and Sue found herself suddenly pregnant with Mike's child. This is where Mike showed his true colors, denying that the child she was carrying was his and dumping her on the spot. Apparently he wasn't as in love with her as everyone thought. Completely crushed, Sue slipped into a state of depression and spent most of her time crying in her room. When she did venture out, it was only to attend class, where she would simply sit and stare at Mike.

As it would happen, Mike met another girl who was almost as pretty as Sue and immediately took up with her, giving no thought at all to Sue and how it might affect her. The other girl lived at Pleasant Hall as well, on the second floor, so it goes without saying that it didn't take long for word to get back to Sue that the love of her life and father of her soon-to-be-born child was shacking up with this girl every weekend. Tempers flared and accusations were tossed about, and Sue made it known to the other girl that if she couldn't have Mike, then no one could. No one really took the threat seriously; they all thought she was just venting.

One Saturday, Mike was sneaking in to see his new girlfriend, and as they got settled in and comfy in her room, the door suddenly flew open, and there stood one highly agitated and irrational Sue. As the argument began, Mike's new love interest got between them, apparently to stake her claim and fight for her man. The argument escalated to a shoving match that ended with Sue pulling a rather large kitchen knife from the folds of her dress and shoving it through the other girl's neck, clear to the hilt. Blood sprayed as she pulled the knife free, and a stunned Mike just stood there as she turned her wrath on him, stabbing him repeatedly in the stomach and chest. When it was over, it was said that he had been stabbed over forty times.

Sue reportedly came back to her senses, realizing what she had done and that her life was over. She ran back up to her room on the third floor, opened the window and leaped to her death.

Over the years, many people have reported seeing a girl falling from a third-floor window and disappearing before hitting the ground. Others have reported waking up to find a blood-covered girl, a gaping wound in her neck, standing at the end of their beds with her arms outstretched and a wild-eyed look on her face.

Pleasant Hall is now a series of classrooms; however, stories are still told about various rooms in the building in which things will move on their own, cries are heard coming from empty rooms and voices will be heard as if someone is whispering in your ear. All in all, it's just another college love story gone bad.

THE HANGING TREE

There is a large, old oak tree on campus (the location of the tree seems to change with each person's telling of the tale) that was the site of a hazing gone bad. One of the fraternities was inducting a new group of pledges, and one of the trials and tribulations that the new guys had to endure was one of unwavering blind trust in their fellow fraternity brothers. After a night of good-natured but sometimes rough hazing, the initiates were brought to this majestic old tree and were told that they were to be hanged by the neck for a few moments and that they had to trust in their frat brothers to cut them down, the message being that you had to trust your brothers with your life.

The young men watched as nooses were thrown over a huge branch of the old tree, and without a doubt, each of them was feeling just a bit worried at the prospect of being strung up by the neck. As they were blindfolded and their hands tied behind their backs, it was explained to them that the ropes would be slipped over their necks and that a group of their brothers would haul them up for a moment and then let them back down. The ropes were put in place, and everyone steeled themselves for what was to come. A group of three guys per rope would pull the initiate up for a fast three-count and then let him back down, where another guy was waiting to loosen the rope and welcome them to the brotherhood. On a count of three, they hauled them up, and after the quick three-counts, they released the ropes—only one rope didn't go back down. Apparently, when the rope was thrown over the branch, it laid next to another smaller branch and when it was pulled up, it became firmly wedged, keeping the unfortunate guy in the air, slowly choking to death.

Frantically, they tried to dislodge the rope, several of the other boys grabbing the hanging one's legs and trying to hold him up until someone could get the rope loose. Finally, someone had enough sense to cut the rope, but by then it was too late. Too much damage had been done to the boy's windpipe, and he died there under the tree. Scared out of their wits, the other guys quickly removed any trace of the rope and the dead boy's blindfold, swore each other to secrecy and ran away as quickly as they could, leaving the dead boy laying there on the grass. It would be the next morning before he was found.

People claim that late at night, when the moon is full and bright, you can see him hanging from the branch, slowly swinging back and forth. It's also been claimed that he haunts the fraternity house, angry that he placed his trust and his life in the hands of those who were not worthy enough to have it.

CONCLUSION

I hope that you have enjoyed reading this book as much as I enjoyed researching and writing it. If you liked this book, I would encourage you to check out my other books, *Haunted Natchez Trace* and *Haunted Mississippi Gulf Coast*, both available from The History Press or your favorite bookseller. I would also ask that you take a moment to check out my website at www. budsteed.com, where you can find other stories I have written, links to my newsletters and my blog and links to Facebook and other social media sites where you can connect with me. I would also ask that you take a moment and go to www.amazon.com and write a review about my books, good or

The Masonic lodge in Baton Rouge is said to be haunted by former members. *Photo by Hope Steed Kennedy.*

bad, so that others might have a better understanding of what my work is about. I thank you in advance and appreciate each and every one of you.

Baton Rouge has a wonderful haunted history, and these are but a few of the stories it has to share. A second and, possibly, third book could be written about all of the alleged hauntings in the Baton Rouge area before one would run out of stories. With such a long and rich history and with so many different cultural making Baton Rouge what it is today, it is little wonder that there are as many stories of ghosts and hauntings as there are. Who would want to leave such a place?

BIBLIOGRAPHY

BOOKS

Armstrong, Annabelle M. *Historic Neighborhoods of Baton Rouge*. Charleston, SC: The History Press, 2010.

Dawson, Sarah Morgan. *A Confederate Girl's Diary*. Chapel Hill: University of North Carolina at Chapel Hill, 1913. Digital edition dated 1997 can be found at www.docsouth.unc.edu/fpn/dawson/dawson.html.

Krousel, Hilda S., PhD. *Landmarks and Monuments of Baton Rouge*. Charleston, SC: The History Press, 2012.

Meyers, Rose. *A History of Baton Rouge, 1699–1812*. Baton Rouge: Louisiana State University Press, 1976.

West Baton Rouge Historical Association. *The History of West Baton Rouge Parish: People, Places, Progress*. St. Louis, MO: Reedy Press, 2012.

ONLINE SOURCES

Baton Rouge Recreation and Park Commission. "Magnolia Mound Plantation." www.brec.org/index.cfm/park/detail/112.

Cathedral of St. Joseph. "History." www.cathedralofstjoseph.org/aboutus/history.

City-Data.com. "Baton Rouge: History." www.city-data.com/us-cities/The-South/Baton-Rouge-History.html.

Dig Baton Rouge. "Haunted Baton Rouge." www.digbatonrouge.com/article/haunted-baton-rouge-5956/.

ExploreSouthernHistory.com. "Baton Rouge National Cemetery." www.exploresouthernhistory.com/batonrougenc.html.

———. "Historic Old Powder Magazine." www.exploresouthernhistory.com/powdermagazine.html

Friends of Magnolia Mound. "The Plantation and Its History." www.friendsofmagnoliamound.org/history.html.

HauntedRouge.com. Is the Doctor In? BR General Hospital." www.hauntedrouge.com/2009/06/is-the-doctor-in-br-general-hospital/.

Historical Baton Rouge. "St. James Episcopal Church." www.historicalbatonrouge.blogspot.com/2009/02/saint-james-episcopal.

Karen's Orphans and Forgotten Residents. "Hard Labor, History and Archaeology at the Louisiana State Penitentiary, Baton Rouge, Louisiana." www.karensorphans.net/pen.htm.

LouisianaOldStateCapitol.org. "History." www.louisianaoldstatecapitol.org/pagedisplay.asp?p1=805&PF=Y.

National Park Service. "Magnolia Mound Plantation." www.nps.gov/nr/travel/louisiana/mag.htm.

———. "Old Louisiana State Capitol." www.nps.gov/nr/travel/louisiana/ocap.htm.

NBC33TV. "Louisiana's Haunted History: Eclipse of the Spanish Moon." www.nbc33tv.com/news/louisianas-haunted-history-eclipse-of-the-spanish-moon.

BIBLIOGRAPHY

Roman Catholic Diocese of Baton Rouge. "History." http://www.diobr. org/index.php?option=com_content&view=article&id=17&Itemid=23.

St. James Episcopal Church. "Who We Are." www.stjamesbr.org/who-we-are.html.

TheShadowLands.net. "Haunted Places in Louisiana." www. theshadowlands.net/places/louisiana.htm.

USS Kidd Veterans Memorial. "History of the USS Kidd." www.usskidd.com.

Waymarking.com. "St. James Episcopal Church." www.waymarking.com/ waymarks/WM781V_St_James_Episcopal_Church_Baton_Rouge_ Louisiana.

Wikipedia.org. "Baton Rouge." http://en.wikipedia.org/wiki/Baton_rouge.

———. "Pentagon Barracks." http://en.wikipedia.org/wiki/Pentagon_ Barracks.

ABOUT THE AUTHOR

A published writer and accomplished photographer, Bud Steed, author of *Haunted Natchez Trace*, *Haunted Mississippi Gulf Coast* and *Haunted Baton Rouge*, devotes his time to writing, paranormal investigations and historical research into potentially haunted sites.

Currently the investigation manager for The Ozarks Paranormal Society (TOPS), based in southwest Missouri, Bud assisted TOPS with the investigation of the Wilson's Creek National Battlefield and the historic Ray House. The investigation was filmed by the Travel Channel for its series *Legends of the Ozarks* and produced startling evidence of hauntings at Wilson's Creek.

Bud has spent much of his time traveling, including living in Germany and France, as well as touring most of Europe while in the army. He has also lived in nine different states since leaving his home in Ohio in 1979. Bud currently lives near Springfield, Missouri, with his wife, Jennifer, and their four children: David, Sean, Ciara Jo and Kerra.

Bud is available for events, book signings and speaking engagements and can be contacted at bud@budsteed.com.

Visit us at
www.historypress.net
....
This title is also available as an e-book